JUDAS ISCARIOT

JUDAS ISCARIOT

by

H. B. DICKEY

"Then said Jesus unto him, That thou doest, do quickly.

"He then having received the sop went immediately out."

—John 13:27, 30

Exposition Press   *New York*

EXPOSITION PRESS INC.

50 Jericho Turnpike   Jericho, New York 11753

FIRST EDITION

0-682-47165-8

Dedicated with reverence to
the Holy Ghost,
the spirit of truth

"And I will pray the Father, and he shall give you another Comforter, that he may abide with you forever;

"Even the Spirit of truth . . .

". . . the Comforter, which is the Holy Ghost . . ."
—John 14:16–17,26

Contents

List of Tables

Prologue

ABOUT MID-CENTURY, while reading the Gospel according to St. John in the King James Version of the Holy Bible, I received a strong, sharp mental impression about Judas Iscariot, one so unique and startling that it has persisted with clarity up to this day. First set down on paper in May, 1965, in the form of an unpublished article, it has eventuated in this volume— further focused thought and additional research for which were initiated on Easter Day, 1969.

If one recalls the words attributed to the Christ by Matthew (10:26): ". . . . for there is nothing covered, that shall not be revealed; and hid, that shall not be known," it is conceivable that the original idea upon which this book is predicated presents a glimpse behind the veil of the One Truth.

Some of the concepts stated herein may or may not be based upon fact. Whether or not suggested hypotheses have scriptural or other validity will depend—at this point in time and space—upon the biblical interpretation, the reasoning ability, and the intuition of the reader.

This work is intended neither to convince nor to convert. It is designed solely to be exploratory in nature and provocative of further thought.

H. B. D.

July 25, 1969

The Lord Buddha Has Said

. . . that we must not believe in a thing said merely because it is said; nor traditions because they have been handed down from antiquity; nor rumors, as such; nor writings by sages, because sages wrote them; nor fancies that we may suspect to have been inspired in us by a Deva (that is, in presumed spiritual inspiration); nor from inferences drawn from some haphazard assumption we may have made; nor because of what seems an analogical necessity; nor on the mere authority of our teachers or masters. But we are to believe when the writing, doctrine, or saying is corroborated by our own reason and consciousness. "For this," he says in concluding, "I taught you not to believe merely because you have heard, but when you believed of your consciousness, then to act accordingly and abundantly."

—H. P. Blavatsky,
The Secret Doctrine (3d ed.) Vol. III p. 401;
quoted by permission of the Theosophical Publishing House,
Adyar, Madras, India

Negative Polarity

Who is Judas? What is he,
That all mankind condemns him?
Master of disloyalty?
Tradition this aspect lends him,
That it might rejected be.

Was he shrewd or was he weak,
The villain of that hour?
How and what did Judas seek—
The silver, or more power?
Or did he deem the Christ too meek?

Hearing, did he hear truth not?
Or see the teaching darkly?
Reason twists, self causes rot,
Reactions strike back starkly.
Who bore the bag still bears the blot.

"Woe to Judas! Better he
Had not been born." What purpose?
Betrayers, thieves in some degree,
Are men, beneath the surface.
Let such seeds ejected be!

Are we shrewd or are we weak,
We humans of this hour?
How and what is it we seek—
More money, or more power?
Or do we deem the Christ too meek?

Hearing, yet we hear truth not.
We see through glamoured glasses.
Mind distorts. Hate causes clot.
Love lacking, wisdom passes.
We bear the bag and wear the blot.

Thanks to Judas! It was he
Who dramatized in action,
Symbolized, and gave the key
To prototype transaction.
Thus he said, "Don't follow me!"

—H B. Dickey

May 24, 1969

JUDAS ISCARIOT

CHAPTER 1

Who Is Judas?

. . . God hath set forth us the apostles last, as it were appointed to death; for we are made a spectacle unto the world, and to angels, and to men. —I CORINTHIANS 4:9

OF THE Twelve Apostles of the Christ and His seventy (or one hundred and twenty) disciples, perhaps none has been made more a "spectacle unto the world" than Judas Iscariot. For nearly two thousand years his act of betrayal has been the nucleus around which a thought-form has been built, until today the very mention of his name evokes contempt. For twenty centuries he has been the target of either hatred or prejudgment.

It is generally accepted that Judas Iscariot symbolizes the lower or personality nature of man, with its affinity for matter, its weaknesses of character, its exaltation of the finite self, and its relation to so-called evil through a tendency to "sin."

It can be said that in the New Testament drama of redemption Jesus and Judas portray parts which might be conceived as polar opposites. Countless books and sermons have pointed out the exemplification in Jesus of the Will of God and the personification in Judas of the will of unregenerate man.

Since its written presentation, that part of the story of Christ's life which deals with the betrayal has been construed in possibly as many ways as there were states of interpreting consciousness. In addition to all of the many theological contentions concerning Judas, there have been various fictional and esoteric explanations. This study is attempted in the light of the intuition in addition to that provided by the Scriptures, reason and outer authorities.

It is perhaps well first to examine the question "Who is Judas?"

All that is currently known of this historical figure is given in the Bible. Among such references, John 6:71 and 13:26 identify him as "Judas Iscariot, the son of Simon." He is said to be a man from Kerioth, a town or city in Judaea, and is believed to be the only one of the twelve apostles who was not a Galilean. (Kerioth is also mentioned in Joshua 15:25.)

The name Judas seems to have been widely used in biblical days. The word itself is said to be a Greek form of the Hebrew Judah, which means "praised."

There are in the Old Testament and the Apocrypha Judas the son of Jacob (also referred to in Matt. 1:2, 3); Judas Maccabaeus (I Macc. 2:1–5), who founded the Maccabees; Judas the son of Chalphi, an army commander associated with Jonathan at Hazor (I Macc. 11:70); Judas the son of Simon Maccabaeus, who, with his brother John, led an army (I Macc. 16:2); the Judas in Jerusalem mentioned in II Maccabees 1:10; and the Judas referred to in I Esdras 9:23 (cf. Ezra 10:23).

In addition to Judas Iscariot, there are several men called Judas in the New Testament: Judas the brother of James, one of the Twelve (Luke 6:16), who is thought to be the Lebbaeus or Thaddaeus of Matthew 10:3, the Thaddaeus of Mark 3:18, and the Judas of John 14:22; Judas the brother of Jesus (Matt. 13:55; Juda, Mark 6:3; Jude, verse 1); Judas the Galilean (Acts 5:37); Judas, the Damascus Jew on the "street called Straight" (Acts 9:11); and Judas Barsabas, who was called a prophet and who accompanied Paul to the churches of Syria and Cilicia (Acts 15:22–33).

It is to be noted that in the various listings of the Twelve Apostles, Judas Iscariot always is mentioned last. Gospel writers identified him by using either the words "Iscariot" or "Simon's son" or "which also betrayed him" in order to distinguish him from Judas the brother of James, who also was one of the Twelve.

Of his life before having been called to service by Jesus, no more is said of Judas Iscariot in the Scriptures than of the other disciples. Aside from details given in the Gospels concerning him prior to and during the betrayal (which will be compared and examined with care), nothing else is said about him.

Neither his stature nor his physical appearance is set forth by Matthew, Mark, Luke, or John. (Despite the absence of such information, Judas has been described in detail by some writers —even to his height, the color of his hair and beard, and the "evil leer" upon his face.) Nor do the authors of the Gospels describe the character or the personality of Judas: his mental processes or his emotional nature, with one exception. This exception may be found in the following statement in John 12:4–6:

> Then saith one of his disciples, Judas Iscariot, Simon's son, which should betray him,
> Why was not this ointment sold for three hundred pence, and given to the poor?
> This he said, not that he cared for the poor; but because he was a thief, and had the bag, and bare what was put therein.

This is a flat statement without supporting evidence of any kind. One has only the word of the author of the Gospel according to St. John, who, unless it was omitted either through error or by deliberation, gave no explanation for such serious charges as hardheartedness and theft.

Today no newspaper, periodical, or other publication in the United States (and possibly in many other countries) would print such an unequivocal accusation without qualification, documentary evidence, witnesses, or an official court verdict, for fear of incurring a suit for slander.

Nowhere else in the Scriptures is such a statement made or implied about Judas. Betrayal, yes. Theft, no. It may, indeed, be true that he was a thief; but is it not curious that this appellation remains unexplained in John and is lacking totally in the other three Gospels? The seeming explanation that Judas "had the bag, and bare what was put therein" explains nothing.

There are perhaps hundreds of thousands of people all over the world who "bear the bag" in the sense that money is entrusted to them for safekeeping and/or distribution; yet this fact alone does not merit their being called either insensitive to the needs of others, or thieves. One wonders if the last verse of the quotation was not slipped in by some overzealous scribe or translator in the very early centuries of the Christian era.

Perhaps because he is said to have betrayed the Christ and to have been a thief, numerous other undesirable characteristics have been attributed to Judas. The temptation to use him as a convenient scapegoat must have proved irresistible to many writers. It is so like man who, if he dislikes a person, group, or nation for one or two negative traits, immediately assigns to that individual, group, or nation every despicable quality imaginable.

Some writers and biblical commentators have stated their personal opinions of Judas Iscariot in such a way that these opinions appear to be facts. Should their readers be interested sufficiently to check the Bible, they could find no verification for statements to the effect that (1) Judas's greedy financial tendencies fed on the thought that Christ planned to usher in a political state over which He would be king and Judas secretary of the treasury; (2) Judas held resentment over having been "rebuked" during the alabaster-box incident; (3) he justified his act of betrayal by believing that if Christ were the Messiah He could not be harmed, but if He were an impostor, the sooner it was known the better, etc.

No such statements are to be found in the Bible. They are the suppositions of men who, of course, have every right to suppose but no right to palm off such guesswork as fact. By so doing they unwittingly or intentionally are misleading their readers and are contributing to the monstrous thought-form that has been built around Judas Iscariot over the centuries.

Aside then from his name and that of his father, nothing actually is known of Judas except that he was chosen as one of the Twelve and that it is written that ultimately he betrayed his Master, returned the thirty pieces of silver to the Temple, and committed suicide.

Such are the facts as presented in the New Testament.

All else that has been said about him either is fictional embroidery or personal opinion, both of which are branches of the tree of imagination. It is true that in the present volume also, opinion and suggestion concerning Judas will be given—but it will be clearly labeled as such. No attempt will be made to present the views of the author as anything other than the views of the author. For after considerable search—aside from the unembellished references in the New Testament itself—one fact has been discovered:

Judas Iscariot is today—after almost two thousand years—still very much a "man of mystery."

CHAPTER 2

The Labor of the Apostles

And as ye go, preach, saying, The kingdom of heaven is at hand. Heal the sick, cleanse the lepers, raise the dead, cast out devils. . . . —MATTHEW 10:7, 8

How WERE the Twelve Apostles chosen?

Jesus must have known the spiritual potential or development of certain men because, during His early travels following His baptism by John, it is written that He said to some, "Follow me." Now, did the first twelve men whom He recognized and called, or who recognized Him and followed, automatically become the Twelve Apostles? Or did the selection of the Twelve result after considerable thought and prayer? Apparently the second, for in Luke (6:12, 13) it is stated:

> And it came to pass in those days that he went out into a mountain to pray, and continued all night in prayer to God.
> And when it was day, he called unto him his disciples: and of them he chose twelve whom he also named apostles . . .

The inference is that during the night He had asked for, and had received, guidance concerning who—out of all the disciples following Him—should be chosen. It is to be noted that this is a deduction, for it is not explicitly so stated. What *is* stated is that He "continued all night in prayer." The content of His prayers is not given. The next verse shows Him choosing the apostles. Because of the proximity of the two concepts, it is presumed that some or all of that particular night was spent in prayer concerning this matter.

Yet in John (2:24, 25) are the definite statements "he knew

all men" and "he knew what was in man." Also in John (16:30) His disciples said to Him: ". . . thou knowest all things." And in Acts (1:24) the disciples' prayer begins: "Thou, Lord, which knowest the hearts of all men . . ."

If it is granted, as all true Christians agree, that Christ knows all things and what is in men's hearts, then does it not follow that He knew the future and what was in the heart of Judas Iscariot?

The names of the Twelve Apostles are listed in three of the Gospels. The Gospel of John does not include the story of the calling or naming of the Twelve. (See Table I, "Choosing the Twelve.") Eleven names are repeated in all three—including that of Judas Iscariot, who is mentioned last—and regarding the identity of only one man is there an apparent discrepancy. Matthew calls one apostle "Lebbaeus, surnamed Thaddaeus." Mark lists him simply as "Thaddaeus." Luke, however, mentions neither Lebbaeus nor Thaddaeus but refers to "Judas, the brother of James."

The point to be established is that Judas Iscariot definitely was chosen by Jesus as one of the Twelve Apostles. There can be no doubt about this, inasmuch as Matthew, Mark, and Luke all mention him in their listings by his two names, together with identifying phrases, as follows: ". . and Judas Iscariot who also betrayed him" (Matt. 10:4); "and Judas Iscariot, which also betrayed him" (Mark 3:19), and "Judas Iscariot, which also was the traitor" (Luke 6:16).

Referring to Table 11, "The Twelve Sent Forth; They Return, Telling All They Had Done," it is interesting to note what it was that these twelve men were authorized to do.

Matthew states that Jesus *gave them power against unclean spirits, to cast them out, and to heal all manner of sickness and all manner of disease.* He quotes the Master as having commanded them, saying, "And as ye go, *preach,* saying the kingdom of heaven is at hand. *Heal the sick, cleanse the lepers, raise the dead, cast out devils. . . ."*

Mark says, "And he *ordained* twelve, that they should be

Table 1

Choosing the Twelve

MATTHEW 10:1–8

1 And when he had called unto him his twelve disciples, he gave them power against unclean spirits, to cast them out, and to heal all manner of sickness and all manner of disease.

2 Now the names of the twelve apostles are these; The first, Simon, who is called Peter, and Andrew his brother; James the son of Zebedee, and John his brother;

3 Philip, and Bartholomew; Thomas, and Matthew the publican; James the son of Alphaeus, and Lebbaeus, whose surname was Thaddaeus;

4 Simon the Canaanite, and Judas Iscariot, who also betrayed him.

5 These twelve Jesus sent forth, and commanded them, saying, Go not into the way of the Gentiles, and into any city of the Samaritans enter ye not.

6 But go rather to the lost sheep of the house of Israel.

7 And as ye go, preach, saying, The kingdom of heaven is at hand.

8 Heal the sick, cleanse the lepers, raise the dead, cast out devils: freely ye have received, freely give.

MARK 3:13–19

13 And he goeth up into a mountain, and calleth unto him whom he would: and they came unto him.

14 And he ordained twelve, that they should be with him, and that he might send them forth to preach.

15 And to have power to heal sicknesses, and to cast out devils:

16 And Simon he surnamed Peter;

17 And James the son of Zebedee, and John the brother of James; and he surnamed them Boanerges, which is, The sons of Thunder;

18 And Andrew, and Philip, and Bartholomew, and Matthew, and Thomas, and James the son of Alphaeus, and Thaddaeus, and Simon the Canaanite,

19 And Judas Iscariot, which also betrayed him: and they went into an house.

LUKE 6:12–16

12 And it came to pass in those days, that he went out into a mountain to pray, and continued all night in prayer to God.

13 And when it was day, he called unto him his disciples: and of them he chose twelve, whom also he named apostles;

14 Simon, (whom he also named Peter,) and Andrew his brother, James and John, Philip and Bartholomew,

15 Matthew and Thomas, James the son of Alphaeus, and Simon called Zelotes,

16 And Judas the brother of James, and Judas Iscariot, which also was the traitor.

JOHN 0

with him, and that he might send them forth to *preach. And to have power to heal sicknesses and to cast out devils.* . . . And he called unto him the twelve and began to send them forth two by two and *gave them power over unclean spirits.* . . ."

In Luke it is recorded: "Then he called his twelve disciples together and *gave them power and authority over all devils, and to cure diseases.* And he sent them forth to *preach . . . and to heal the sick.* . . ."[1]

Need one call to mind that Judas Iscariot, being one of the Twelve, was ordained for the above labor, as were the other eleven Apostles? He, too, may have preached and cast out devils and healed the sick.

Jesus sent them forth "two by two," according to Mark; therefore it is to be expected that some of those persons who abhor Judas for the betrayal either have stated, or will conclude, that the apostle who accompanied Judas Iscariot did all of the preaching, healing, and casting out of devils. But such would be prejudice, pure and simple. For the King James Version of the Bible states exactly what is given in the accompanying tables and does not specify what any one Apostle did or did not do.

From the story it is more reasonable to deduce that Judas participated to some degree in all of these activities, for he too had been ordained and therefore was qualified fully to perform such services. And if he had neglected for any reason to do so, is it not strange that there is no record of his having thus shirked?

About their journeys, Mark writes: ". . . and they went out and *preached* . . . and they *cast out many devils and anointed with oil many that were sick, and healed them.*" And Luke says: "And they departed and went through the towns, *preaching the gospel and healing every where.*"

Assuming, for the sake of argument, that Judas Iscariot did none of these things, it still must be admitted that he was a

---

[1] Unless otherwise stated, all biblical quotations in this volume are from the King James Version. (The italics are mine—H. B. D.)

member of the inner group, that he traveled with them, that he heard the words of the Master and saw the miracles that were performed by Him and by at least one of His Apostles. (For even if Judas himself did no preaching or healing or casting out of devils, he was sent forth with a partner who must have been thus engaged.)

In short, Judas Iscariot was exposed not only to the teaching but to the Teacher and to the physical-plane effects of His power for at least two full years. A portion of His power and authority had been transmitted to Judas, as to the other eleven. Judas, along with the rest of the inner group, had been—except for those times when they were sent forth to heal, to preach, or on various other missions—within the immediate aura (or electromagnetic field) of the Master during most of His main ministry.

Is it then reasonable that Judas could have been the only one to remain unaffected by the positive emanations pouring forth from the "Son of man"? The strength of these radiations was so great that a woman, who had been diseased with an issue of blood for twelve years and who had faith, was cured instantly as a result of having touched the border of His garment (Matt. 9:20; Mark 5:25; Luke 8:43).

Could Judas, any more than the others, have thought Jesus to be an impostor or clever magician, as some writers have suggested? If any one of the Apostles was prone to serious doubt, might it not have been Thomas? He has become so famous for that quality that people, to this very day, say of many a Tom, Dick, or Harry: "He's a doubting Thomas."

Objectors immediately will bring forward Satan. "It is not," they will say, "necessarily true that Judas doubted that Christ was the Messiah but rather that Satan entered into Judas later, planting doubts and ideas which caused him to betray our Lord." This scripturally authenticated viewpoint will be considered in a later chapter, after all relevant Gospel references to Judas have been examined and compared.

Then what happened, after the Twelve returned?

Mark (6:30) reports: "And the apostles gathered themselves

Table II

THE TWELVE SENT FORTH;

THEY RETURN, TELLING ALL THEY HAD DONE

MATTHEW 10:1,7–10

1 And when he had called unto him his twelve disciples, he gave them power against unclean spirits, to cast them out, and to heal all manner of sickness and all manner of disease.

7 And as ye go, preach, saying, The kingdom of heaven is at hand.

8 Heal the sick, cleanse the lepers, raise the dead, cast out devils: freely ye have received, freely give.

9 Provide neither gold, nor silver, nor brass in your purses,

10 Nor scrip, for your journey, neither two coats, neither shoes, nor yet staves: for the workman is worthy of his meat.

MARK 6:7–9,12,13,30–32

7 And he called unto him the twelve, and began to send them forth by two and two; and gave them power over unclean spirits;

8 And commanded them that they should take nothing for their journey, save a staff only; no scrip, no bread, no money in their purse:

9 But be shod with sandals; and not put on two coats.

12 And they went out, and preached that men should repent.

13 And they cast out many devils, and anointed with oil many that were sick, and healed them.

30 And the apostles gathered themselves together unto Jesus, and told him all things, both what they had done, and what they had taught.

31 And he said unto them, Come ye yourselves apart into a desert place, and rest a while: for there were many coming and going, and they had no leisure so much as to eat.

32 And they departed into a desert place by ship privately.

LUKE 9:1-3,6,10

1 Then he called his twelve disciples together, and gave them power and authority over all devils, and to cure diseases.

2 And he sent them to preach the kingdom of God, and to heal the sick.

3 And he said unto them, Take nothing for your journey, neither staves, nor scrip, neither bread, neither money; neither have two coats apiece.

6 And they departed, and went through the towns, preaching the gospel, and healing everywhere.

10 And the apostles, when they were returned, told him all that they had done. And he took them, and went aside privately into a desert place belonging to the city called Bethsaida.

JOHN 0

together unto Jesus and told him all things, both what they had done and what they had taught." Luke (9:10) says simply: "And the apostles, when they were returned, told him all that they had done." No exceptions or omissions are mentioned.

Suffice it to say (1) that Judas Iscariot was selected deliberately by Jesus—as were eleven other men—to be one of the Twelve Apostles; (2) that he, like each of them, was given power and authority to preach that the kingdom of heaven was at hand, to heal the sick, to cleanse the lepers, to cast out devils, and to raise the dead; and (3) that he was sent forth with the others so to do.

Such are the facts up to this point, as given in the Bible. All else is supposition.

CHAPTER 3

Jesus Foretells His Death and Judas Confers With the Priests

". . . having ears, hear ye not?"   —MARK 8:18

PROBABLY many people read straight through one chapter of the Bible at a time. Biblical students unquestionably pause to check center-references or to refer to concordances concerning persons or subjects in which they are interested. Almost everyone knows about or is familiar with a tabulation that is called *The Harmony of the Gospels,* wherein the contents of the story of Christ's life are arranged as chronologically as is possible in the left-hand column, while to the right are shown in which Gospels, chapters, and verses various events can be found.

Today many Bibles contain such a harmony, which usually is located in the back of the book, with supplementary information such as miracles, parables, definitions of terms, summary of the books of the Bible, notes on geography, maps, etc.

But one wonders how many readers have been sufficiently curious about Judas Iscariot to have developed tables of comparison, as it were, so that each Evangelist's telling of any given incident relevant to Judas might better be studied and analyzed. Such a method would immediately call attention to many details that might go undetected, were each Gospel portion read alone or were a student checking back and forth concerning some one point.

For the convenience of both author and reader, this has been done: there are nine such tables in this volume, all based on verbatim quotations from the King James Version of the Holy Bible—although several other translations were examined diligently.

Table III relates to the first time the Master prophesied His death and resurrection. This telling occurred at Caesarea Philippi. The second time He made this prediction was in Galilee, as shown in Table IV. He spoke on the same subject a third time while He and His disciples were "going up to Jerusalem," as given in Table V. Only Matthew briefly cites a fourth reminder concerning His death (but not His resurrection) in Table VI. All of these announcements preceded the Master's prediction about betrayal that was made during the Last Supper.

Referring first to Table III, one notices that the words "delivered" and "betrayed" are conspicuous by their absence.

Matthew (16:21) says: "From that time forth *began* Jesus to shew unto his disciples, how that he must go unto Jerusalem, and suffer many things of the elders and chief priests and scribes, and be killed, and be raised again the third day."

In Mark (8:31) it is stated: "And he *began* to teach them, that the Son of man must suffer many things, and be rejected of the elders, and of the chief priests, and scribes, and be killed, and after three days rise again."

While the report of Luke (9:22) reads thus: ". . . The Son of man must suffer many things, and be rejected of the elders and chief priests and scribes, and be slain, and be raised the third day."

Matthew uses the word "shew" ("show"), while Mark says "teach."

At this early stage, Simon Peter attempted to remonstrate with Jesus, saying (Matt. 16:22): "Be it far from thee, Lord: this shall not be unto thee"; whereupon Jesus turned and said to Peter: "Get thee behind me, Satan: thou art an offense unto me: for thou savourest not the things that be of God, but those that be of men." Mark (8:33) substantiates this almost word for word.

Now while almost everyone recalls and refers to the italicized portions of the following statements, taken from Luke (22:3,4) *"Then entered Satan into Judas surnamed Iscariot, being of the* number of the twelve. And he went his way, and communed with the chief priests and captains, how he might betray him unto them," and from John (13:26,27): ". . . And when he had dipped the sop, he gave it to Judas Iscariot, the son of Simon. And *after the sop Satan entered into him*"—there appears to be little or no emphasis on the fact that it was Peter to whom the Lord said, "Get thee behind me, Satan."

In either event, with reference to both Peter and Judas, Satan is the personification of the principle of testing. Peter's remarks could be interpreted as constituting a form of temptation to Jesus, while the sop given to Judas may have some connection with temptation in regard to the Twelfth Apostle.

Immediately after the Master's announcement about—and discussion pertaining to—His death, He began to talk about one of the basic requirements for discipleship, in the following manner: ". . . If any man will come after me, let him deny himself, and take up his cross, and follow me. For whosoever will save his life shall lose it: and whosoever will lose his life for my sake shall find it. For what is a man profited, if he gain the whole world, and lose his own soul? or what shall a man give in exchange for his soul?" (Matt. 16:24-26.) Except for a slight difference in wording, exactly the same idea is expressed by both Mark and Luke.

Another thought mentioned next in the Scriptures (probably because it belongs exactly there) has, because of it unusualness, been included in Table III. Matthew, Mark, and Luke are in accord insofar as the substance of the concept is concerned:

> MATTHEW (16:28): Verily I say unto you, There shall be some standing here, which shall not taste of death, till they see the Son of man coming in his kingdom.
> MARK (9:1): . . . Verily I say unto you, That there be some of them that stand here, which shall not taste of death, till they have seen the kingdom of God come with power.
> LUKE (9:27): But I tell you of a truth, there be some standing here, which shall not taste of death, till they see the kingdom of God.

Table III

THE FIRST TIME JESUS FORETELLS HIS DEATH
AND RESURRECTION (At Caesarea Philippi)

MATTHEW 16:21–28	MARK 8:31–36;9:1
21 From that time forth began Jesus to shew unto his disciples, how that he must go unto Jerusalem, and suffer many things of the elders and chief priests and scribes, and be killed, and be raised again the third day.	31 And he began to teach them, that the Son of man must suffer many things, and be rejected of the elders, and of the chief priests, and scribes, and be killed, and after three days rise again.
22 Then Peter took him, and began to rebuke him, saying, Be it far from thee, Lord: this shall not be unto thee.	32 And he spake that saying openly. And Peter took him, and began to rebuke him.
23 But he turned, and said unto Peter, Get thee behind me, Satan: thou art an offence unto me: for thou savourest not the things that be of God, but those that be of men.	33 But when he had turned about and looked on his disciples, he rebuked Peter, saying, Get thee behind me, Satan; for thou savourest not the things that be of God, but the things that be of men.
24 Then said Jesus unto his disciples, If any man will come after me, let him deny himself, and take up his cross, and follow me.	34 And when he had called the people unto him with his disciples also, he said unto them, Whosoever will come after me, let him deny himself, and take up his cross, and follow me.
25 For whosoever will save his life shall lose it: and whosoever will lose his life for my sake shall find it.	35 For whosoever will save his life shall lose it: but whosoever shall lose his life for my sake and the gospel's, the same shall save it.
26 For what is a man profited, if he shall gain the whole world, and lose his own soul? or what shall a man give in exchange for his soul?	36 For what shall it profit a man, if he shall gain the whole world, and lose his own soul?
27 For the Son of man shall come in the glory of his Father with his angels; and then he shall reward every man according to his works.	1 And he said unto them, Verily I say unto you, That there be some of them that stand here, which shall not taste of death, till they have seen the kingdom of God come with power.
28 Verily, I say unto you, There be some standing here, which shall not taste of death, till they see the Son of man coming in his kingdom.	

LUKE 9:22–25,27   **JOHN 0**

22 Saying, The Son of man must suffer many things, and be rejected of the elders and chief priests and scribes, and be slain, and be raised the third day.

23 And he said to them all, If any man will come after me, let him deny himself, and take up his cross daily, and follow me.

24 For whosoever will save his life shall lose it: but whosoever will lose his life for my sake, the same shall save it.

25 For what is a man advantaged, if he gain the whole world, and lose himself, or be cast away?

27 But I tell you of a truth, there be some standing here, which shall not taste of death, till they see the kingdom of God.

There also is reference to this idea in the last verses of the last chapter of the Gospel according to St. John.

According to certain authorities, the above events are purported to have taken place at Caesarea Philippi sometime between April and October in the year A.D. 29. The second time that Jesus foretold His death and resurrection, He and His disciples were around Galilee (see Table IV). This took place during the same general month-span, but after the Transfiguration.

It is during this second prophecy that the word "betrayed" first appears (Matt. 17:22). In both Mark (9:31) and Luke (9:44) Jesus is quoted as having used the word "delivered."

Matthew treats this occasion briefly—in two verses—and ends by saying (17:23): "And they were exceeding sorry."

Mark (9:32) states: "But they understood not that saying, and were afraid to ask him." Could this have been because they recalled how sharply Peter had been rebuked when the same subject had been brought up earlier?

However, Luke (9:45) says a curious thing: "But they understood not this saying, and it was hid from them, that they perceived it not: and they feared to ask him that saying." Exactly what saying was hidden from them, that they perceived it not? In the previous verse in Luke, the Master is said to have stated: "Let these sayings sink down into your ears: for the Son of man shall be *delivered* into the hands of men." Was that so difficult of comprehension?

In Mark (9:31) it is spelled out more clearly: "The Son of man is *delivered* into the hands of men, and they shall kill him; and after that he is killed, he shall rise the third day."

Surely the Apostles and disciples were reasonably intelligent people. They must have been familiar with the meaning of the word "delivered." They would have linked it with "turned over to the authorities." And people—far earlier than two thousand years ago—were aware of what happens when a man or an animal is killed: an inert, insensitive, unseeing, unhearing, unfeeling, unknowing physical body remains and decays after the life principle has fled. The disciples must, at some time or other, have seen or have heard about so-called death. Therefore, by a process of elimination, the saying that was "hid from them, that they perceived it not" must have been that which concerned Christ's rising again on the third day. According to biblical scholars, Lazarus had not been raised at that time. The raising of Lazarus is placed between the following January and March in the year A.D. 30.

This particular foretelling is followed immediately by a dispute among the disciples about who would be greatest among them (Mark 9:34: Luke 9:46). Whereupon Jesus is credited with the following statement: ". . . If any man desire to be first, the same shall be last of all, and servant of all" (Mark 9:35) or, as Luke (9:48) puts it, ". . . for he that is least among you all, the same shall be great." On the surface these words seem readily understandable: i.e., that discipleship is based upon selfless service and genuine humility (which latter term has been defined as "an adjusted sense of right proportion"). But is there meaning beneath the surface?

Going up to Jerusalem during what has been estimated as the month of March in A.D. 30 (presumably after the raising of Lazarus), Jesus foretold His death and resurrection a third time. (See Table V.)

Again both Mark and Luke use the word "delivered" and again Matthew says "betrayed." In this instance, the Master goes into far more detail than He did on the two previous occasions. A glance at Table V will show that He used highly colorful words which should have left no doubt about what He was saying.

For example, in Matthew (20:18,19): "Behold, we go up to Jerusalem; and the Son of man shall be *betrayed* unto the chief priests and unto the scribes, and they shall condemn him to death. And shall deliver him to the Gentiles to mock, and to scourge, and to crucify him: and the third day he shall rise again."

Mark's rendition of what Jesus said could not have been

Table IV

THE SECOND TIME JESUS FORETELLS HIS DEATH
AND RESURRECTION (In Galilee)

MATTHEW 17:22–23

22 And while they abode in Galilee, Jesus said unto them, The Son of man shall be betrayed into the hands of men:

23 And they shall kill him, and the third day he shall be raised again. And they were exceeding sorry.

MARK 9:30–35

30 And they departed thence and passed through Galilee; and he would not that any man should know it.

31 For he taught his disciples, and said unto them, The Son of man is delivered into the hands of men, and they shall kill him; and after that he is killed, he shall rise the third day.

32 But they understood not that saying, and were afraid to ask him.

33 And he came to Capernaum: and being in the house he asked them, What was it that ye disputed among yourselves by the way?

34 But they held their peace: for by the way they had disputed among themselves, who should be the greatest.

35 And he sat down, and called the twelve, and saith unto them, If any man desire to be first, the same shall be last of all, and servant of all.

LUKE 9:43–46,48

43 And they were all amazed at the mighty power of God. But while they wondered every one at all things which Jesus did, he said unto his disciples,

44 Let these sayings sink down into your ears: for the Son of man shall be delivered into the hands of men.

45 But they understood not this saying, and it was hid from them, that they perceived it not: and they feared to ask him of that saying.

46 Then there arose a reasoning among them, which of them should be greatest.

48 And said unto them . . . for he that is least among you all, the same shall be great.

JOHN 0

Table V

THE THIRD TIME JESUS FORETELLS HIS DEATH
AND RESURRECTION (Going Up to Jerusalem)

MATTHEW 20:17–19,26–28

17 And Jesus going up to Jerusalem took the twelve disciples apart in the way, and said unto them,

18 Behold, we go up to Jerusalem; and the Son of man shall be betrayed unto the chief priests and unto the scribes, and they shall condemn him to death,

19 And shall deliver him to the Gentiles to mock, and to scourge, and to crucify him: and the third day he shall rise again.

26 . . . but whosoever will be great among you, let him be your minister;

27 And whosoever will be chief among you, let him be your servant:

28 Even as the Son of man came not to be ministered unto, but to minister, and to give his life a ransom for many.

MARK 10:31–34,43–45

31 But many that are first shall be last; and the last first.

32 And they were in the way going up to Jerusalem; and Jesus went before them: and they were amazed; and as they followed, they were afraid. And he took again the twelve, and began to tell them what things should happen unto him,

33 Saying, Behold, we go up to Jerusalem; and the Son of man shall be delivered unto the chief priests, and unto the scribes; and they shall condemn him to death, and shall deliver him to the Gentiles:

34 And they shall mock him, and shall scourge him, and shall spit upon him, and shall kill him: and the third day he shall rise again.

43 But so shall it not be among you: but whosoever will be great among you, shall be your minister:

44 And whosoever of you will be the chiefest, shall be the servant of all.

45 For even the Son of man came not to be ministered unto, but to minister, and to give his life a ransom for many.

LUKE 18:31–34   JOHN 0

31 Then he took unto him the twelve, and said unto them, Behold, we go up to Jerusalem, and all things that are written by the prophets concerning the Son of man shall be accomplished.

32 For he shall be delivered unto the Gentiles, and shall be mocked, and spitefully entreated, and spitted on:

33 And they shall scourge him, and put him to death: and the third day he shall rise again.

34 And they understood none of these things: and this saying was hid from them, neither knew they the things which were spoken.

more direct: ". . . Behold, we go up to Jerusalem; and the Son
of man shall be *delivered* unto the chief priests, and unto the
scribes; and they shall condemn him to death, and shall deliver
him to the Gentiles. And they shall mock him, and shall scourge
him, and shall spit upon him and shall kill him: and the third
day he shall rise again." (Mark 10:33,34.)

Luke (18:31–33) seems equally clear: ". . . Behold, we go
up to Jerusalem, and all things that are written by the prophets
concerning the Son of man shall be accomplished. For he shall
be *delivered* unto the Gentiles, and shall be mocked, and spitefully entreated, and spitted on: And they shall scourge him, and
put him to death: and the third day he shall rise again."

Luke however, again insists in the same chapter, next verse,
that "they understood none of these things: and this saying was
hid from them, neither knew they the things which were
spoken."

Now, since nothing could have been worded more simply
or directly (in all three Gospel reports), and since some biblical
scholars, if not all, place the time of this particular prophecy *after*
the raising of Lazarus, what possibly could have been hidden
from their understanding?

Could it have been that Luke himself did not comprehend
because he did not want these things to happen to his Lord?
People hear what they want to hear. Might that not have been
the case with some of the others? Indeed, lack of understanding
in this matter could have been due to some such psychological
blocking. Or were the disciples paying no attention at the time?

It is questionable to assume, as some persons have, that the
Christ never intended that His disciples should understand this
prophecy. If that were the case, then why—as Luke himself reported earlier (9:44)—did the Lord say: "Let these sayings sink
down into your ears"? Or why did He spend so much of His
time and energy telling them essentially the same thing on at
least three different occasions?

It is more logical to believe that the difficulty was within
the disciples themselves: in their minds, perhaps; but more likely

in their emotional natures. At a much earlier date, in speaking to them, the Christ is quoted as having said: "Why reason ye because ye have no bread? perceive ye not yet, neither understand? have ye your heart yet hardened? Having eyes, see ye not? and having ears, hear ye not? and do ye not remember?" (Mark 8:17,18.)

Undoubtedly when Luke said that "they understood none of these things" he believed sincerely that he was speaking for them all. As perhaps he was. Yet is it not conceivable that some of the Apostles might have understood, at least to some degree, "the things that were spoken"? (That this was a possibility, one has only to recall Peter's reaction the first time the prediction was made.)

It is to be noted that shortly after Jesus prophesied His death for the third time, He again explained that "whoever will be great among you, let him be your minister," etc. (Matt. 20:26; Mark 10:43).

Among other things, Table VI cites the fourth time that Jesus foretold His death, when He was seated talking to His disciples on the Mount of Olives. He mentioned it in passing, as it were, and did not refer to the resurrection. The report is very brief—one verse—and is given only in Matthew (26:2). The balance of this table primarily concerns the conference of Judas with the chief priests and scribes.

In the relating of Christ's prophecies concerning His death, Matthew's is the only Gospel in which there is a definite reference to crucifixion. The first and second times the story is told, Matthew uses the words "killed" and "kill"; the third and fourth times he says "crucify" and "crucified."

As may be verified by reference either to the Bible or to Tables III, IV, and V, Mark uses the words "killed," "kill" and "condemn to death," while Luke chooses "be slain" and "put to death."

Next to be examined is how Judas is said to have consulted with the chief priests, as shown in Table VI.

Table VI   THE FOURTH TIME JESUS FORETELLS HIS DEATH
(On the Mount of Olives)
JUDAS CONFERS WITH THE CHIEF PRIESTS

MATTHEW 26:1–5,14–19

1 And it came to pass, when Jesus had finished all these sayings, he said unto his disciples,
2 Ye know that after two days is the feast of the passover, and the Son of man is betrayed to be crucified.
3 Then assembled together the chief priests, and the scribes, and the elders of the people, unto the palace of the high priest, who was called Caiaphas,
4 And consulted that they might take Jesus by subtilty, and kill him.
5 But they said, Not on the feast day, lest there be an uproar among the people.
14 Then one of the twelve, called Judas Iscariot, went unto the chief priests,
15 And said unto them, What will ye give me, and I will deliver him unto you? And they covenanted with him for thirty pieces of silver.
16 And from that time he sought opportunity to betray him.
17 Now the first day of the feast of unleavened bread the disciples came to Jesus, saying unto him, Where wilt thou that we prepare for thee to eat the passover?
18 And he said, Go into the city to such a man, and say unto him, The Master saith, My time is at hand; I will keep the passover at thy house with my disciples.
19 And the disciples did as Jesus had appointed them; and they made ready the passover.

MARK 14:1,2,10–13,16

1 After two days was the feast of the passover, and of unleavened bread; and the chief priests and the scribes sought how they might take him by craft, and put him to death.
2 But they said, Not on the feast day, lest there be an uproar of the people.
10 And Judas Iscariot, one of the twelve, went unto the chief priests, to betray him unto them.
11 And when they heard it, they were glad, and promised to give him money. And he sought how he might conveniently betray him.
12 And the first day of unleavened bread, when they killed the passover, his disciples said unto him, Where wilt thou that we go and prepare that thou mayest eat the passover?
13 And he sendeth forth two of his disciples, and saith unto them, Go ye into the city, and there shall meet you a man bearing a pitcher of water: ° follow him.
16 And his disciples went forth, and came into the city, and found as he had said unto them: and they made ready the passover.

°The Zodiac symbol of Aquarius is a man bearing a pitcher of water.

LUKE 22:1–10,13

1 Now the feast of unleavened bread drew nigh, which is called the Passover.

2 And the chief priests and scribes sought how they might kill him; for they feared the people.

3 Then entered Satan into Judas surnamed Iscariot, being of the number of the twelve.

4 And he went his way, and communed with the chief priests and captains, how he might betray him unto them.

5 And they were glad, and covenanted to give him money.

6 And he promised, and sought opportunity to betray him unto them in the absence of the multitude.

7 Then came the day of unleavened bread, when the passover must be killed.

8 And he sent Peter and John, saying, Go and prepare us the passover, that we may eat.

9 And they said unto him, Where wilt thou that we prepare?

10 And he said unto them, Behold, when ye are entered into the city, there shall a man meet you, bearing a pitcher of water; follow him into the house where he entereth in.*

13 And they went, and found as he had said unto them: and they made ready the passover.

JOHN 12:23,32,33

23 And Jesus answered them, saying, The hour is come, that the Son of man should be glorified.

32 And I, if I be lifted up from the earth, will draw all men unto me.

33 This he said, signifying what death he should die.

*The Zodiac symbol of Aquarius is a man bearing a pitcher of water.

Before the Passover, the chief priests and scribes discussed how they might put Jesus to death. They decided not to attempt it on the feast day for fear of an uproar among the people. Meanwhile in Bethany, while Jesus sat eating, a woman is said to have arrived with an alabaster box containing a very precious ointment, which she had brought for the purpose of anointing Him.

What happened at this point is told somewhat differently in the various Gospels. Matthew (26:8,9) says that when His disciples saw this, "*they* had indignation, saying, To what purpose is this waste? For this ointment might have been sold for much, and given to the poor." Mark (14:4,5) agrees: "And there were *some* that had indignation among themselves, and said, Why was this waste of the ointment made? For it might have been sold for more than three hundred pence, and have been given to the poor. And *they* murmured against her."

Luke does not mention the incident, and John has a variation on the theme.

Matthew and Mark place this happening *two* days before the Passover, while John says that *six* days prior to the Passover Jesus went to Bethany. But to quote John (12:1–6):

> Then Jesus six days before the passover came to Bethany, where Lazarus was which had been dead, whom he raised from the dead.
> There they made him a supper; and Martha served: but Lazarus was one of them that sat at the table with him.
> Then took Mary a pound of ointment of spikenard, very costly, and anointed the feet of Jesus, and wiped his feet with her hair: and the house was filled with the odour of the ointment.
> Then saith one of his disciples, Judas Iscariot, Simon's son, which should betray him,
> Why was not this ointment sold for three hundred pence, and given to the poor?
> This he said, not that he cared for the poor; but because he was a thief, and had the bag, and bare what was put therein.

In passing, it is interesting to note that not only do Matthew

and Mark disagree with John as to timing, but they do not
identify the woman with the alabaster box. And both of them
state that she poured its contents on the head of Jesus, whereas
John says that she anointed His feet.

Since neither Matthew nor Mark states that Judas was
present, some authorities have concluded that it was while
Jesus was in Bethany thus engaged that Judas availed himself
of the Master's retirement to covenant with the chief priests to
betray Him.

John, however—by identifying Judas as the one to make
objection to the use of the costly ointment (although Matthew
credits this objection to "his disciples" and Mark to "some")—
thereby definitely places Judas Iscariot in Bethany with Jesus
during the alabaster box incident.

Immediately following this story, Matthew (26:14) and
Mark (14:10) begin to describe the activity of Judas and his
discussion with the priests.

Luke (22:1-7), as stated above, omits the tale of the pouring of the ointment entirely and, in speaking of the conference
of Judas, brings Satan into the picture:

> Now the feast of unleavened bread drew nigh, which is
> called the Passover.
> And the chief priests and scribes sought how they might kill
> him: for they feared the people.
> Then entered Satan into Judas surnamed Iscariot, being of
> the number of the twelve.
> And he went his way, and communed with the chief priests
> and captains, how he might betray him unto them.
> And they were glad, and covenanted to give him money.
> And he promised, and sought opportunity to betray him unto
> them in the absence of the multitude.
> Then came the day of unleavened bread, when the passover
> must be killed.

The important thing to note here is that Judas Iscariot is
said to have made arrangements for the betrayal at least two
days *prior* to the Last Supper. This is called to attention because

—due to the wording in John (13:27), "And *after* the sop Satan entered into him"—it often has been believed that the entire betrayal took place *following* the sop. Also, John omits any mention of a previous conference between Judas and the priests.

The other Gospels, however, tell this story in some detail, including the monetary arrangements (thirty pieces of silver) that were agreed upon. Matthew, Mark, and Luke all place the betrayal conference between Judas and the chief priests *prior* to the Last Supper.

To recapitulate the major concepts considered in this chapter:

In Matthew, Jesus is said to have foretold His death on four separate occasions; in Mark and Luke, three different times. So goes the written record. Who among men really knows how often the Master discussed this subject with His Apostles? The law of averages alone would suggest that as a result of all of these seed-thoughts, the basic idea might have found lodgment in the mind or heart of at least one of the Twelve.

And after close examination and comparison of the four Gospels relevant to the events pertaining to Judas Iscariot thus far, the question may be asked: When did Judas covenant to betray the Lord, *before* or *after* the Last Supper?

CHAPTER 4

Judas Is Present During the Last Supper

Likewise also the cup after supper, saying, This cup is the new testament in my blood, which is shed for you.
But, behold, the hand of him that betrayeth me is with me on the table. —LUKE 22:20,21

THERE ARE devoted Christians who would like to believe—and doubtless many do—that since Judas is said to have betrayed the Lord, he was not entitled to partake of the bread and the wine and must have left the Upper Room before the Christ instituted the ritual that has come to be known as the Last Supper.

Nowhere in the Scriptures is it even suggested that Judas Iscariot left before the bread and the wine, as will be seen by referring to the comparisons set forth in Table VII.

However, since neither Matthew nor Mark says when Judas departed (or even *if* he departed), and since both quote Jesus as mentioning the betrayal prior to giving the bread and wine to His apostles, the field is left open, as it were, for speculation. Hence people have speculated.

There are Christians who read and quote whichever Gospel best appears to support their personal theories and pay little or no attention to anything that might seem to refute them. Human beings have a tendency to believe what they want to believe, all evidence to the contrary notwithstanding. One wonders, for example, how many persons have compared the following corresponding verses in Matthew and Mark.

Matthew (26:27), in reporting the words of Jesus, states: "And he took the cup and gave thanks, and gave it to them, saying, *Drink ye all* of it." Whereas Mark (14:23) says: "And

Table VII Jesus Refers to the One Who Shall Betray Him

(At the Last Supper)

MATTHEW 26:20–30	MARK 14:17–26
20 Now when the even was come, he sat down with the twelve.	17 And in the evening he cometh with the twelve.
21 And as they did eat, he said, Verily I say unto you, that one of you shall betray me.	18 And as they sat and did eat, Jesus said, Verily I say unto you, One of you which eateth with me shall betray me.
22 And they were exceeding sorrowful, and began every one of them to say unto him, Lord, is it I?	19 And they began to be sorrowful, and to say unto him one by one, Is it I? and another said, Is it I?
23 And he answered and said, He that dippeth his hand with me in the dish, the same shall betray me.	20 And he answered and said unto them, It is one of the twelve, that dippeth with me in the dish.
24 The Son of man goeth as it is written of him: but woe unto that man by whom the Son of man is betrayed! it had been good for that man if he had not been born.	21 The Son of man indeed goeth, as it is written of him: but woe to that man by whom the Son of man is betrayed! good were it for that man if he had never been born.
25 Then Judas, which betrayed him, answered and said, Master, is it I? He said unto him, Thou hast said.	22 And as they did eat, Jesus took bread, and blessed, and brake it, and gave to them, and said, Take, eat: this is my body.
26 And as they were eating, Jesus took bread, and blessed it, and brake it, and gave it to the disciples, and said, Take, eat; this is my body.	23 And he took the cup, and when he had given thanks, he gave it to them: and they all drank of it.
27 And he took the cup, and gave thanks, and gave it to them, saying, Drink ye all of it;	24 And he said unto them, This is my blood of the new testament, which is shed for many.
28 For this is my blood of the new testament, which is shed for many for the remission of sins.	25 Verily, I say unto you, I will drink no more of the fruit of the vine, until that day that I drink it new in the kingdom of God.
29 But I say unto you, I will not drink henceforth of this fruit of the vine, until that day when I drink it new with you in my Father's kingdom.	26 And when they had sung an hymn, they went out into the mount of Olives.

14 And when the hour was come, he sat down, and the twelve apostles with him.

15 And he said unto them, With desire I have desired to eat this passover with you before I suffer:

16 For I say unto you, I will not any more eat thereof, until it be fulfilled in the kingdom of God.

17 And he took the cup, and gave thanks, and said, Take this, and divide it among yourselves:

18 For I say unto you, I will not drink of the fruit of the vine, until the kingdom of God shall come.

19 And he took bread, and gave thanks, and brake it, and gave unto them, saying, This is my body which is given for you: this do in remembrance of me.

20 Likewise also the cup after supper, saying, This cup is the new testament in my blood, which is shed for you.

21 But, behold, the hand of him that betrayeth me is with me on the table.

22 And truly the Son of man goeth, as it was determined: but woe unto that man by whom he is betrayed!

23 And they began to inquire among themselves, which of them it was that should do this thing.

24 And there was also a strife among them, which of them should be accounted the greatest.

25 And he said unto them, the kings of the Gentiles exercise lordship over them; and they that exercise authority upon them are called benefactors.

1 Now before the feast of the passover, when Jesus knew that his hour was come that he should depart out of this world unto the Father, having loved his own which were in the world, he loved them unto the end.

2 And supper being ended, the devil having now put into the heart of Judas Iscariot, Simon's son, to betray him;

3 Jesus knowing that the Father had given all things into his hands, and that he was come from God, and went to God;

4 He riseth from supper, and laid aside his garments; and took a towel, and girded himself.

5 After that he poureth water into a basin, and began to wash the disciples' feet, and to wipe them with the towel wherewith he was girded.

9 Simon Peter saith unto him, Lord, not my feet only, but also my hands and my head.

10 Jesus saith to him, He that is washed needeth not save to wash his feet, but is clean every whit: and ye are clean, but not all.

15 For I have given you an example, that ye should do as I have done to you.

16 Verily, verily, I say unto you, The servant is not greater than his lord; neither he that is sent greater than he that sent him.

17 If ye know these things, happy are ye if ye do them.

18 I speak not of you all: I know whom I have chosen: but that the scripture may be fulfilled, He that eateth bread with me

30 And when they had sung an
hymn, they went out into the
mount of Olives.

26 But ye shall not be so: but he that is greatest among you, let him be as the younger; and he that is chief, as he that doth serve.

27 For whether is greater, he that sitteth at meat, or he that serveth? Is not he that sitteth at meat? but I am among you as he that serveth.

28 Ye are they which have continued with me in my temptations.

29 And I appoint unto you a kingdom as my Father hath appointed unto me;

30 That ye may eat and drink at my table in my kingdom, and sit on thrones judging the twelve tribes of Israel.

hath lifted up his heel against me.

21 When Jesus had thus said, he was troubled in spirit, and testified, and said, Verily, verily, I say unto you, that one of you shall betray me.

22 Then the disciples looked one on another, doubting of whom he spake.

23 Now there was leaning on Jesus' bosom one of his disciples, whom Jesus loved.

24 Simon Peter therefore beckoned to him, that he should ask who it should be of whom he spake.

25 He then lying on Jesus' breast saith unto him, Lord, who is it?

26 Jesus answered, He it is, to whom I shall give a sop, when I have dipped it. And when he had dipped the sop, he gave it to Judas Iscariot, the son of Simon.

27 And after the sop Satan entered into him. Then said Jesus unto him, That thou doest, do quickly.

28 Now no man at the table knew for what intent he spake this unto him.

29 For some of them thought, because Judas had the bag, that Jesus had said unto him, Buy those things that we have need of against the feast; or, that he should give something to the poor.

30 He then having received the sop went immediately out: and it was night.

31 Therefore, when he was gone out, Jesus said, Now is the Son of man glorified, and God is glorified in him.

he took the cup, and when he had given thanks, he gave it to them: and *they all drank* of it."

Because of the different positions of three similar words, the entire meaning appears to be changed. Almost everyone thinks that "drink ye all of it" is a command not to leave one drop in the chalice. However, if the same words are read with another intonation, the thought changes:, i.e., drink, ye all, of it. Hence it could be interpreted in the sense: ye all drink of it. Inflected in this manner, it would be in line with Mark's wording: "they all drank of it."

Mark's rendition that "they all drank of it" implies the presence of Judas Iscariot but is not, in itself, irrefutable proof. It is not a statement of that fact; it merely suggests or implies it.

However, provided the Scriptures are considered as the final authority and as such are believed to be without error, the Gospel according to St. Luke (22:19-21) provides indisputable evidence that Judas Iscariot was present during the Last Supper:

> And he took bread, and gave thanks, and brake it, and gave unto them, saying, This is my body which is given for you: this do in remembrance of me.
> Likewise also the cup after supper, saying, This cup is the new testament in my blood, which is shed for you.
> But, behold, the hand of him that betrayeth me is with me on the table.

In this presentation it is definitely not until *after* the bread and the wine are given to the Apostles that Jesus states: "But, behold, the hand of him that betrayeth me is with me on the table."

John does not refer to the giving of the bread and wine so that, although he speaks in some detail about the sop and subsequent departure of Judas, one cannot deduce at which point the Twelfth Apostle left in relation to this ritual.

At this point in Luke (22:23)—immediately following the

Master's reference to His betrayer—the disciples "began to enquire among themselves which of them it was that should do this thing. And there was also a strife among them, which of them should be accounted greatest."

Is it not indeed strange, to say the least, that at a time of such great gravity they should be arguing about precedence and over their own importance? One could say that they did not yet realize that this was the moment about which Jesus had several times spoken. They could be defended on the grounds that they were little different from most members of the human race who, after almost two thousand years, still are self-centered even in so-called spiritual matters. Either or both of which arguments may indeed be true. But this was not the first time they had worried over their greatness.

Earlier, en route between Galilee and Capernaum, shortly after Jesus' second prophecy about His death and resurrection (Table IV), both Mark and Luke state that the disciples disputed among themselves concerning who should be greatest. And even then, it is difficult to imagine why they, following such a serious prediction about their Teacher, should have been debating about their future glory.

It may have been that they felt that it would be needful for someone to head the group, should Jesus some day be killed as He had foretold, and they merely were wondering which of them it might be. Or perhaps the subject was a natural consequence of Jesus' prior statement that some who stood there would not "taste of death" until they had seen the Son of man and the kingdom of God coming with great power (Table III: Matt. 16:28; Mark 9:1; Luke 9:27).

In any event, in answer to their disputations, it is said that Jesus told the Twelve: "If any man desire to be first, the same shall be last of all and servant of all" (Mark 9:35). This theme He reiterated on several occasions.

And He is said to have repeated essentially the same idea during the Last Supper following the strife between the Apostles about which of them should be considered the greatest. Luke (22:26) quotes Him as having said: ". . . he that is greatest among you, let him be as the younger; and he that is chief, as he that doth serve."

It is here in Luke's Gospel that a statement is made, the full significance of which has been all but overlooked. Jesus, in talking with His Apostles, is purported to have said (Luke 22:28–30):

> Ye are they which have continued with me in my temptations.
> And I appoint unto you a kingdom, as my Father has appointed unto me;
> That ye may eat and drink at my table in my kingdom, and sit on thrones judging the *twelve* tribes of Israel.

Notice the word "twelve." Would He have mentioned judging twelve tribes to eleven men? Is it not more likely that He was talking to all the Twelve?

But someone will immediately object, because Judas Iscariot was one of the Twelve. And did Judas not betray his Master? It is perhaps well to consider this objection and the possible alternatives.

One person might inquire, "Would not the Christ himself have completed the twelve judges?" Since it was He who was appointing unto each of them a kingdom, a place at His table, thrones, and authority to judge the twelve tribes, this alternative seems unreasonable: He was their spiritual superior.

Someone else will ask, "What about the replacement for Judas? Perhaps Our Lord had in mind Matthias, who later was to be 'numbered with the eleven apostles'?" This suggestion surely should not be ruled out as a possibility.

But it is well to keep in mind that the Bible does not say either that Judas Iscariot was absent when Jesus was speaking or that Jesus was thinking in terms of Matthias. Such alternatives constitute conjectures. They would be the products of human minds, the suppositions of persons who were not witnesses.

Luke does not state when Judas left the Upper Room, or

even whether or not he left before the others. From his Gospel it is known that Judas Iscariot was present during the ritual of the bread and wine. Judas may—or may not—have been there when Jesus appointed unto each of the apostles a kingdom. Certainly he was one of the inner group who had continued with the Teacher throughout His major ministry.

All that is known to men—at this point in time and space— is that Luke records that after supper the Christ addressed His apostles, as quoted above, and that He said that they would "sit on thrones judging the *twelve* tribes of Israel."

In John (13:2) there is another implication that Judas was present during the Last Supper: "And *supper being ended,* the devil having *now* put into the heart of Judas Iscariot, Simon's son, to betray him . . ." The wording here can but mean that it was *after* the Last Supper that the "devil" put the betrayal idea into Judas's heart.

At first glance it is not entirely clear whether or not Judas was present during the foot washing (Table VII). However, a rereading of John 13:10—"He that is washed needeth not save to wash his feet, but is clean every whit: and ye are clean, but not all"—and of John 13:18—"I speak not of you all: I know whom I have chosen: but that the scripture may be fulfilled, He that eateth bread with me hath lifted up his heel against me."— leaves one with the impression that He was speaking to all Twelve. If so, Judas was one whose feet Jesus washed.

This deduction is strengthened in John (13:21): "When Jesus had thus said, he was troubled in spirit, and testified, and said, Verily, verily, I say unto you that one of you shall betray me."

Apparently the Apostles, at that point, were not aware which of them it would be, for it is written that they looked at one another "doubting of whom he spake." Whereupon Peter beckoned to the disciple who was "leaning on Jesus' bosom" (the one "Jesus loved") to make inquiry—which he did. In reply to the question, "Lord, who is it?" Jesus is said to have stated, "He it is to whom I shall give a sop when I have dipped it."

The balance of the quotation taken from the Gospel of St. John
(13:26–31), as shown in Table VII, is given below:

> . . . And when he had dipped the sop, he gave it to Judas
> Iscariot, the son of Simon.
> And after the sop Satan entered into him. Then Jesus said
> unto him, That thou doest, do quickly.
> Now no man at the table knew for what intent he spake this
> unto him.
> For some of them thought, because Judas had the bag, that
> Jesus had said unto him, Buy those things that we have need of
> against the feast; or, that he should give something to the poor.
> He then having received the sop went immediately out: and
> it was night.
> Therefore, when he was gone out, Jesus said, Now is the
> Son of man glorified, and God is glorified in him.

Because of the sentence "And after the sop Satan entered
into him," some persons think that Judas Iscariot made the
arrangements for the betrayal that same night, after which he
guided the officers of the chief priests to the Mount of Olives,
where he identified Jesus for them. Such people, however, may
be overlooking the statements of Matthew (26:14–16), Mark
(14:1,2; 10,11), and Luke (22:1–6), as given in Table VI.
These Gospels go into some detail about the conference between Judas and the chief priests, placing it two days before
the feast of the unleavened bread, called the Passover, and
hence prior to the Last Supper. At the conclusion of their reports
concerning this discussion Matthew (26:16) states: "And from
that time he sought opportunity to betray him"; Mark (14:11)
says: "And he sought how he might conveniently betray him";
while Luke (22:6) words the idea thus: "And he promised and
sought opportunity to betray him unto them in the absence of
the multitude."

It is a matter, is it not, of how the word "betray" is defined?
Surely covenanting with the priests for money was, in itself, a
form of betrayal as the word ordinarily is used. Depending,
therefore, upon the meaning intended, there may exist no con-

tradition between John's rendition and the conference stories in the other three Gospels.

If by betrayal is meant only the *act* of identifying Jesus, then betrayal occurred after the sop, as John indicates. However, if by betrayal one includes the *intention* of so doing, the *planning* thereof, and the *seeking of opportunity* (in addition to the *act* of identification), then Judas may be said to have betrayed his Lord at least two days in advance of the Last Supper.

It is interesting to note that, while John states that Satan entered into Judas after the sop, Luke says that Satan entered into him much earlier (as a result of which, it is implied, he went to confer with the priests).

To a modern scholar the term "Satan" itself needs defining. Possible meanings of this word will be investigated in a later chapter.

Reverting to John (13:28,29)—"Now no man at the table knew for what intent he spake this unto him. For some of them thought, because Judas had the bag, that Jesus had said unto him, Buy those things that we have need of against the feast; or, that he should give something to the poor"—one wonders why the Apostles thought either of these things.

Such lack of comprehension is difficult to reconcile with other facts given in the same chapter: i.e., that Jesus had just announced that one of them would betray Him; that they had looked at one another "doubting of whom he spake"; that Peter had beckoned to another disciple, urging him to ask the Master which of them it would be; that the disciple had so asked; that Jesus had replied, "He it is to whom I shall give a sop when I have dipped it"; and that Judas was the man to whom the sop was given.

Apparent discrepancies and puzzling statements in the Gospels of Matthew, Mark, Luke, and John may be due as much to their authors' knowledge, points of consciousness, and skill in revealing truth (while simultaneously veiling it) as to errors resulting from the multifarious interpretations of copiers and translators or to possible editing of early church councils.

Also, such seeming contradictions may be due to the amount of knowledge, point of consciousness, or degree of intuitive discernment of the reader.

For all ideas—spiritual or otherwise—of necessity either must be stepped down by, or passed through, the minds and brains of human receivers. And in so doing they are colored or distorted by the limitations and imperfections of the instruments through which they are transmitted.

CHAPTER 5

In the Garden of Gethsemane

*Jesus, therefore, knowing all things that should come upon him,
went forth and said unto them, Whom seek ye?*   —JOHN 18:4

IT IS RECORDED that after the teaching of the Master on the
occasion of the Last Supper, "when they had sung an hymn,
they went out into the mount of Olives." The Bible then tells
of Jesus praying and three times finding Peter, James, and
John asleep.

Table VIII shows what happened in the Garden of Gethsemane when Jesus was delivered to the officers of the chief
priests. When placed side by side (as in this table), the events
described by the authors of the four Gospels reveal certain dis-
similarities.

For example, Matthew (26:47–50) relates:

> And while he yet spake, lo, Judas, one of the twelve, came,
> and with him a great multitude with swords and staves, from the
> chief priests and elders of the people.
> Now he that had betrayed him gave them a sign, saying
> Whomsoever I shall kiss, that same is he: hold him fast.
> And forthwith he came to Jesus, and said, Hail, Master; and
> kissed him.
> And Jesus said unto him, Friend, wherefore art thou come?
> Then came they, and laid hands on Jesus, and took him.

Mark (14:43–46) states:

> And immediately, while he yet spake, cometh Judas, one of
> the twelve, and with him a great multitude with swords and
> staves, from the chief priests and the scribes and the elders.
> And he that betrayed him had given them a token, saying,
> Whomsoever I shall kiss, that same is he; take him and lead him
> away safely.

Table VIII
JESUS IS DELIVERED TO THE OFFICERS OF THE CHIEF PRIESTS
(In the Garden of Gethsemane)

MATTHEW 26:45-50;53-56

45 Then cometh he to his disciples, and saith unto them, Sleep on now, and take your rest; behold, the hour is at hand, and the Son of man is betrayed into the hands of sinners.
46 Rise, let us be going: behold, he is at hand that doth betray me.
47 And while he yet spake, lo, Judas, one of the twelve, came, and with him a great multitude with swords and staves, from the chief priests and elders of the people.
48 Now he that betrayed him gave them a sign, saying, Whomsoever I shall kiss, that same is he: hold him fast.
49 And forthwith he came to Jesus, and said, Hail, master; and kissed him.
50 And Jesus said unto him, Friend, wherefore art thou come? Then came they, and laid hands on Jesus, and took him.
53 Thinkest thou that I cannot now pray to my Father, and he shall presently give me more than twelve legions of angels?
54 But how then shall the scriptures be fulfilled, that thus it must be?
55 In that same hour said Jesus to the multitudes, Are ye come out as against a thief with swords and staves for to take me? I sat

MARK 14:41-46,48-50

41 And he cometh the third time, and saith unto them, Sleep on now, and take your rest: it is enough, the hour is come; behold, the Son of man is betrayed into the hands of sinners.
42 Rise up, let us go; lo, he that betrayeth me is at hand.
43 And immediately, while he yet spake, cometh Judas, one of the twelve, and with him a great multitude with swords and staves, from the chief priests and the scribes and the elders.
44 And he that betrayed him had given them a token, saying, Whomsoever I shall kiss, that same is he; take him, and lead him away safely.
45 And as soon as he was come, he goeth straightway to him, and saith, Master, master; and kissed him.
46 And they laid their hands on him and took him.
48 And Jesus answered and said unto them, Are ye come out, as against a thief, with swords and with staves to take me?
49 I was daily with you in the temple teaching, and ye took me not: but the scriptures must be fulfilled.
50 And they all forsook him, and fled.

LUKE 22:45–48,52–54

45 And when he rose up from prayer, and was come to his disciples, he found them sleeping for sorrow,

46 And said unto them, Why sleep ye? rise and pray, lest ye enter into temptation.

47 And while he yet spake, behold a multitude, and he that was called Judas, one of the twelve, went before them, and drew near unto Jesus to kiss him.

48 But Jesus said unto him, Judas, betrayest thou the Son of man with a kiss?

52 Then Jesus said unto the chief priests, and captains of the temple, and the elders, which were come to him, Be ye come out, as against a thief, with swords and staves?

53 When I was daily with you in the temple, ye stretched forth no hands against me: but this is your hour, and the power of darkness.

54 Then they took him, and led him, and brought him into the high priest's house. And Peter followed afar off.

JOHN 18:1–9,12–17

1 When Jesus had spoken these words, he went forth with his disciples over the brook Cedron, where was a garden, into the which he entered, and his disciples.

2 And Judas also, which betrayed him, knew the place: for Jesus ofttimes resorted thither with his disciples.

3 Judas then, having received a band of men and officers from the chief priests and Pharisees, cometh thither with lanterns and torches and weapons.

4 Jesus therefore, knowing all things that should come upon him, went forth and said unto them, Whom seek ye?

5 They answered him, Jesus of Nazareth. Jesus saith unto them, I am he. And Judas also, which betrayed him, stood with them.

6 As soon then as he had said unto them, I am he, they went backward, and fell to the ground.

7 Then asked he them again, Whom seek ye? And they said, Jesus of Nazareth.

8 Jesus answered, I have told you that I am he; if therefore ye seek me, let these go their way:

9 That the saying might be fulfilled, which he spake, Of them which thou gavest me have I lost none.

12 Then the band and the cap-

MATTHEW (cont.)
daily with you teaching in the
temple, and ye laid no hold on
me.
56 But all this was done, that
the scriptures of the prophets
might be fulfilled. Then all the
disciples forsook him, and fled.

JOHN (cont.)

tain and officers of the Jews took Jesus, and bound him.

13 And led him away to Annas first; for he was father in law to Caiaphas, which was the high priest that same year.

14 Now Caiaphas was he, which gave counsel to the Jews, that it was expedient that one man should die for the people.

15 And Simon Peter followed Jesus, and so did another disciple: that disciple was known unto the high priest, and went in with Jesus into the palace of the high priest.

16 But Peter stood at the door without. Then went out that other disciple, which was known unto the high priest, and spake unto her that kept the door, and brought in Peter.

17 Then saith the damsel that kept the door unto Peter, Art not thou also one of this man's disciples? He saith, I am not.

And as soon as he was come, he goeth straightway to him, and saith, Master, master; and kissed him.

And they laid their hands on him, and took him.

Luke (22:47,48) says:

And while he yet spake, behold, a multitude, and he that was called Judas, one of the twelve, went before them, and drew near unto Jesus to kiss him.

But Jesus said unto him, Judas, betrayest thou the Son of man with a kiss?

However, John (18:3–9,12,13) differs in his presentation of the same events:

Judas then, having received a band of men and officers from the chief priests and Pharisees, cometh thither with lanterns and torches and weapons.

Jesus therefore, knowing all things that should come upon him, went forth, and said unto them, Whom seek ye?

They answered him, Jesus of Nazareth. Jesus saith unto them, I am he. And Judas also, which betrayed him, stood with them.

As soon then as he had said unto them, I am he, they went backward, and fell to the ground.

Then asked he them again, Whom seek ye? And they said, Jesus of Nazareth.

Jesus answered, I have told you that I am he: if therefore ye seek me, let these go their way:

That the saying might be fulfilled which he spake, Of them which thou gavest me have I lost none. . . .

Then the band and the captain and officers of the Jews took Jesus and bound him,

And led him away to Annas first; for he was father in law to Caiaphas, which was the high priest that same year.

Note that while Matthew says that Judas went to Jesus saying, "Hail, Master," and kissed him (to which Jesus is said to have replied, "Friend, wherefore art thou come?"), Mark has Judas greet Jesus with the words, "Master, master" prior to kissing him (and does not give Jesus' reply). Mark also quotes

Judas as telling the arresting officers to lead Jesus away *safely*. Luke states that Jesus' reaction to the kiss (or to the intended kiss—for Luke does not actually say that Judas kissed Him)— was in the form of the following question: "Judas, betrayest thou the Son of man with a kiss?"

Despite these variations in reporting, the basic story in Matthew, Mark, and Luke is essentially the same: i.e., that the Twelfth Apostle led "a great multitude," armed with swords, staves, lanterns, etc., to the Lord, whereupon Judas gave them an identifying sign or token in the form of a kiss.

However, what appears to be an entirely different tale is told by John. In his Gospel there is apparently not even a remote similarity to the method of identifying Jesus found in Matthew, Mark, and Luke.

John places Judas with the arresting officers and says that Jesus, "knowing all things that should come upon him, went forth and said unto them, Whom seek ye?" When they had answered, *Jesus identified Himself* with the words "I am he." It is then related that as soon as He had said that, "they went backward and fell to the ground." One wonders why. After which He asked the same question a second time and received the same reply, whereupon He said: "I have told you that I am he; if therefore ye seek me, let these go their way." Then the captain and officers of the Jews took Jesus, bound Him, and led Him away.

On the surface, John *appears* to be contradicting the events as told by the writers of the other three Gospels. He may, or may not, be so doing. It is possible that details of the story, as told in John, were omitted by Matthew, Mark, and Luke; and, conversely, that the points cited by Matthew, Mark, and Luke were omitted by John. In other words, there may be no contradiction. (It has been said that there exists no contradiction which can not be resolved.)

It could be assumed that from Jesus emanated an energy or force of such power that the people standing before Him were literally swept from their feet and knocked to the ground.

This, in itself, should have removed any and all doubt concerning His identity and should have charged the minds of all present—especially the minds of those to whom it had happened —with both awe and wonder. For could any human being—without a weapon or so much as a touch—have felled an entire group of men? Can any man do so today?

After the officers "laid their hands on him, and took him," Jesus is credited with the following statements.

According to Matthew (26:53-56):

> Thinkest thou that I cannot now pray to my Father, and he shall presently give me more than twelve legions of angels?
> *But how then shall the scriptures be fulfilled, that thus it must be?*
> In that same hour Jesus said to the multitudes, Are ye come out as against a thief with swords and staves for to take me? I sat daily with you teaching in the temple, and ye laid no hold on me.
> *But all this was done, that the scriptures of the prophets might be fulfilled.* Then all the disciples forsook him and fled.

Mark (14:48-50) reports:

> And Jesus answered and said unto them, Are ye come out, as against a thief, with swords and staves to take me?
> I was daily with you in the temple teaching, and ye took me not: *but the scriptures must be fulfilled.*
> And they all forsook him and fled.

While Luke (22:52-54) has this to say:

> Then Jesus said unto the chief priests, and captains of the temple, and the elders, which were come to him, Be ye come out, as against a thief, with swords and staves?
> When I was daily with you in the temple, ye stretched forth no hands against me: *but this is your hour, and the power of darkness.*
> Then they took him, and led him, and brought him into the high priest's house. And Peter followed afar off.

John does not mention that Jesus remonstrated with the multitude or with the chief priests, captains, and elders, as quoted above, but he does—as do Matthew, Mark, and Luke—discuss Peter at this point. In Table VIII, only a portion of John's reference to Peter has been included. This was done for a reason. Says John (18:14–17):

> Now Caiaphas was he, which gave counsel to the Jews, that it was expedient that one man should die for the people.
> And Simon Peter followed Jesus, and so did another disciple: that disciple was known unto the high priest, and went in with Jesus into the palace of the high priest.
> But Peter stood at the door without. Then went out that other disciple, which was known unto the high priest, and spake unto her that kept the door, and brought in Peter.
> Then saith the damsel that kept the door unto Peter, Art not thou also one of this man's disciples? He saith, I am not.

Who was the other disciple—the one who "went in with Jesus into the palace of the high priest"? Some biblical students believe him to have been John, the beloved Apostle. Others think it may have been one of the seventy. And there is no denying the possibility that it could have been either "a man of the Pharisees, named Nicodemus, a ruler of the Jews," who went to consult with Jesus after nightfall (John 3:1,2) or "Joseph of Arimathaea, being a disciple of Jesus, but secretly for fear of the Jews" (John 19:38), who was a counselor or member of the Sanhedrin, both of whom must have had access to the palace of the high priest.

One wonders if there is a man today who knows the identity of this disciple. Any of the above conjectures could be true. However, there is another possibility that may have been overlooked through the centuries: the other disciple could have been Judas Iscariot.

If so, this might account for the fact that he was not named. No one will disagree when it is said that Judas was "known unto the high priest." Had he not conferred with the chief priests about his Master? Had he not engaged in a business transaction with them? Had he not been the instrument whereby Jesus was delivered to them? Did they not believe that he had turned traitor? Might they not have hoped that he would make various accusations against Jesus? Or provide additional evidence? Perhaps serve as a witness for the prosecution?

Would Nicodemus or Joseph of Arimathaea place himself in the compromising position of going out, speaking to the doorkeeper, and bringing in Peter? Did either of them wish it known that he was a disciple of Jesus?

Which of the Master's other Apostles or disciples would have dared to do such a thing? For by calling in Peter, they would have run the risk of being identified as members of Jesus' group.

Who, among the disciples, was in no danger from the Sanhedrin?

Who—except Judas Iscariot?

The above quotations from Matthew, Mark, and Luke tend to verify the possibility that no one could have taken Jesus into custody had He not permitted it. The reason why He allowed Himself to be captured is made abundantly clear by the statements to the effect that *"all this was done, that the scriptures might be fulfilled."*

There is, however, additional biblical proof to warrant this conclusion. More than once Caiaphas and the Sanhedrin determined to put Jesus to death. And on at least three occasions attempts were made to seize Him, to stone Him, or to kill Him. In John (7:30): "Then they sought to take him, but *no man laid hands on him because his hour was not yet come"*; John (8:20): "These words spake Jesus in the treasury, as he taught in the temple: *and no man laid hands on him: for his hour was not yet come"*; John (8:59): "Then took they up stones to cast at him, but *Jesus hid himself, and went out of the temple, going through the midst of them,* and so passed by"; John (10:39): "Therefore they sought again to take him; but he *escaped out of their hand."*

In all of His travels, among all manner of people, including His enemies, is it "accidental" that Jesus was not harmed? There were plots against His life. Among His listeners there were angry men whose impulse was to pick up rocks from the road and stone Him. Yet strangely "no man laid hands on him because his hour was not yet come." Who or what prevented such men from killing Him? Note especially the wording of the reference wherein He *"hid himself, and went out of the temple, going through the midst of them."* How can a person hide himself by walking straight into and through the very crowd that is seeking to stone him?

Some people would answer that question by suggesting mass hypnosis or by saying that since Jesus was the Son of God, He escaped by performing a miracle.

Now a miracle is a miracle because of its rarity and because the law upon which it is based either is not recognized or is not known. To have hidden Himself while "going through the midst" of His attackers, Jesus might have had to make Himself invisible. In which instance the miracle would have been that of invisibility. How might a physical body be rendered invisible?

How do the solid steel blades of an ordinary electric fan become invisible? The reality and the presence of such blades no one can doubt when the fan is inoperative. But when the electric current is switched on and these same blades begin to rotate, they remain visible for only a few seconds. As they accelerate they become no more than a blur to the eyes of the beholder. At top speed, one cannot see them at all.

Perhaps by using the same basic law—by heightening or increasing the vibration of the cells of His dense physical body to the point of invisibility—Jesus passed through the crowd unseen.

At other times He may have intensified the force-field around Him to form a protective shield so that His enemies could not lay their hands on Him.

If anyone doubts the Christ's ability to handle and control energy, let that person remember John's story about the night in the Garden of Gethsemane when an entire band of men "went backward and fell to the ground" before Him.

Provided that it is granted that Jesus could exercise such power by virtue of the authority vested in Him by the Father (and why should it not be granted, since the Bible states among other things that He healed all manner of diseases, fed multitudes from a few loaves and fishes, cast out devils, raised the dead, walked on water, calmed the elements, and rose from His own sepulchre?), it follows that He could have been arrested by the officers of the chief priests—or not—as He allowed.

One has only to recall His words to Pilate at the trial: "Thou couldest have no power at all against me, except it were given thee from above" (John 19:11).

Such being the case, was there any need for a betrayer?

As He told His captors, He sat daily with them in the Temple, teaching. He also walked the highways and byways of the land for many months, followed sometimes by multitudes. Certainly many people knew Him and easily could have pointed Him out to the religious authorities. Moreover, His enemies had tried to snare Him verbally by means of sophistry and so were conversing with Him face to face.

At one time the chief priests, the scribes, and the elders had assembled in the palace of the high priest, Caiaphas, to consult how "they might take Jesus by subtilty and kill him" (Matt. 26:4). But they did not want to do this on the feast day for fear there would be an uproar among the people.

Instead of making an agreement with Judas to deliver his Master to them, could the chief priests not have had Jesus followed in order to capture Him when He was alone with His disciples?

Perhaps they had tried such a scheme but were not successful for the same reason that others had failed to seize or to stone Him. The Bible does not record or imply any such attempt. But it *could* have been an alternative, had Jesus permitted it. Why was it not used? Or some similar plan?

Why betrayal?

CHAPTER 6

Thirty Pieces of Silver

. . . What is that to us?   —MATTHEW 27:4

QUESTIONS that could occur to some people while reading the quotations from Matthew given in Table IX might include: How did the author of that Gospel know the content of the conversations between Judas and the chief priests? Was Matthew present on those occasions? Or did Judas tell him?

If Judas Iscariot had told Matthew about the conference during which he had agreed to deliver the Master to the priests for thirty pieces of silver, one or more of the Apostles would have realized that Judas was the man to whom Jesus referred when He spoke of a betrayer at the Last Supper. And since it is believed that Judas left the Upper Room before the others in order to lead the arresting officers to the Christ, it is not likely that he engaged in conversation with any of them at that time.

Regarding the verbal exchange that took place when Judas returned the thirty pieces of silver: since the Bible says that Judas left the Temple "and went and hanged himself," it is not reasonable to suppose that he stopped along the way to chat with anyone. A man with such intent would not be in the mood.

A verbal report of these conversations might have passed from someone who was there on both occasions to one of the disciples or to Matthew directly. Or, as an alternative suggestion, there is the very real possibility that the Christ—who knew or could know all things—had, by an extension of His senses of sight and sound, learned what had taken place and had advised one or more of His Apostles.

Moreover, there is a third factor: that of possible error and/or

Table IX
THIRTY PIECES OF SILVER AND THE DEATH OF JUDAS

MATTHEW 26:14–16;27:1–10

14 Then one of the twelve, called Judas Iscariot, went unto the chief priests.

15 And said unto them, What will ye give me, and I will deliver him unto you? And they covenanted with him for thirty pieces of silver.

16 And from that time he sought opportunity to betray him.

1 When the morning was come, all the chief priests and elders of the people took counsel against Jesus to put him to death:

2 And when they had bound him, they led him away, and delivered him to Pontius Pilate the governor.

3 Then Judas, which had betrayed him, when he saw that he was condemned, repented himself, and brought again the thirty pieces of silver to the chief priests and elders,

4 Saying, I have sinned in that I have betrayed the innocent blood. And they said, What is that to us? see thou to that.

5 And he cast down the pieces of silver in the temple, and departed, and went and hanged himself.

6 And the chief priests took the silver pieces, and said, It is not lawful for to put them into the treasury, because it is the price of blood.

7 And they took counsel, and

ACTS 1:16–26

16 Men and brethren, this scripture must needs have been fulfilled, which the Holy Ghost by the mouth of David spake before concerning Judas, which was guide to them that took Jesus.

17 For he was numbered with us, and had obtained part of this ministry.

18 Now this man purchased a field with the reward of iniquity; and falling head long, he burst asunder in the midst, and all his bowels gushed out.

19 And it was known unto all the dwellers at Jerusalem; insomuch as that field is called in their proper tongue, Aceldama, that is to say, The field of blood.

20 For it is written in the book of Psalms, Let his habitation be desolate, and let no man dwell therein: and his bishoprick let another take.

21 Wherefore of these men which have companied with us all the time that the Lord Jesus went in and out among us,

22 Beginning from the baptism of John, unto that same day that he was taken up from us, must one be ordained to be a witness with us of his resurrection.

23 And they appointed two, Joseph called Barsabas, who was surnamed Justus, and Matthias.

24 And they prayed, and said, Thou, Lord, which knowest the

bought with them the potter's field, to bury strangers in.

8 Wherefore that field was called, The field of blood, unto this day.

9 Then was fulfilled that which was spoken by Jeremy the prophet, saying, And they took the thirty pieces of silver, the price of him that was valued, whom they of the children of Israel did value;

10 And gave them for the potter's field, as the Lord appointed me.

hearts of all men, shew whether of these two thou hast chosen,

25 That he may take part of this ministry and apostleship, from which Judas by transgression fell, that he might go to his own place.

26 And they gave forth their lots; and the lot fell upon Matthias; and he was numbered with the eleven apostles.

tampering by those who copied down or translated early documents or by those who later determined which should be included as sacred writings and which were to be considered apocryphal, which hidden, and which destroyed. The possibility of altering, whether accidentally or deliberately, should be recognized in studying any ancient scripture because there were many opportunities for errors, both of omission and of commission.

It is well to keep in mind that as far as is known to Bible scholars at present, Jesus wrote nothing, and it has not been discovered whether anyone was taking notes while the events given in the Gospels occurred.

The content of the Bible that has passed down through the centuries quite possibly is based upon legend, recollection, or divine inspiration. Or a combination thereof. In any event, the information had to filter through one or more human minds. Now, human minds must use human brains as instruments on the physical plane, and since anything strictly human is far from perfect, ideas are distorted even before they are limited by the inadequacies and intricacies of language.

For the reader's convenience, Matthew 27:1-8 is quoted here:

When the morning was come, all the chief priests and elders of the people took counsel against Jesus to put him to death:

And when they had bound him, they led him away, and delivered him to Pontius Pilate the governor.

Then Judas, which had betrayed him, when he saw that he was condemned, repented himself, and brought again the thirty pieces of silver to the chief priests and elders,

Saying, I have sinned in that I have betrayed the innocent blood. And they said, What is that to us? see thou to that.

And he cast down the pieces of silver in the temple, and departed, and went and hanged himself.

And the chief priests took the silver pieces, and said, It is not lawful for to put them into the treasury, because it is the price of blood.

And they took counsel, and bought with them the potter's field, to bury strangers in.

Wherefore that field was called, The field of blood, unto this day.

The chief priests considered the money that Judas had returned to be "the price of blood." In all probability they had received back the same thirty pieces of silver which they had given him. In any event, one wonders if it entered the consciousness of any of them that when they gave the silver to Judas, they were *paying* "the price of blood."

These were supposed to have been men of God, interpreters of the Law, sanctified and holy. What manner of men were they who could scheme and plot to take a person's life in the name of religion? And as if it were not enough for priests to plan a "legalized" murder, they attempted to shift the blame to Judas and the responsibility to Pilate.

In studying this story, one begins to comprehend the depth to which at least part of the priesthood had fallen at that time, and to understand why Jesus is reported by Matthew (23:27) to have said: "Woe unto you, scribes and Pharisees, hypocrites! for ye are like unto whited sepulchres, which indeed appear beautiful outward, but are within full of dead men's bones, and of all uncleanness."

Matthew concludes his record of the activities of Judas by

saying that after he had cast down the silver, he departed "and went and hanged himself." However, Acts (1:18) says that "falling headlong, he burst asunder in the midst, and all of his bowels gushed out." Again, an apparent contradiction. In order to try to reconcile these varying stories, it has been suggested that after Judas had "hanged himself," either the rope or the branch broke, causing him to fall to the ground. Some authorities state that in Greek the words for "being hanged" may mean either "having fallen forward" or perhaps "having swollen up."

The tale about Judas Iscariot ends with the report of his suicide.

After Judas' recorded death, Acts (1:16–26) states that of the two disciples who had been appointed, Matthias was selected to fill the vacancy within the inner council of twelve. Verses 24 and 25 of Acts I read:

> And they prayed, and said, Thou, Lord, which knowest the hearts of all men, shew whether of these two thou hast chosen,
> That he may take part of this ministry and apostleship, from which Judas by transgression fell, that he might go to his own place.

There have been those who have believed the latter part of Verse 25 to mean that it was Judas who "might go to his own place," implying that region ruled by Satan. However, it could be construed that it was Matthias who "might go to his own place" among the Apostles.

It is questionable if anyone in the human kingdom either knows, or is authorized to reveal, the *cause* behind Judas's act of betrayal. But its *effects* still thunder through the centuries.

Someone is certain to point out that Judas's act was included in the redemptive drama in order that one of the Scriptures might be fulfilled. According to John (13:18), Jesus is reported to have said: ". . . I know whom I have chosen: but *that the scripture may be fulfilled*, He that eateth bread with me hath lifted up his heel against me."[2] This reason, given as it is in the New Testament, is undeniable and undebatable. But it does not answer the more basic question, "Why?"

Why, seemingly, was an act of treachery essential to this story about the mission of Jesus? Since it has been noted in the previous chapter that He could have been located and arrested by the officers of the high priests through some method other than that of betrayal, it is perhaps time to analyze this concept seriously.

The subject of betrayal also needs to be examined carefully for the more immediate reason that today countless persons still are giving and taking the symbolic "thirty pieces of silver." Men look upon betrayal at this time as they did two thousand years ago, accusing the person who betrays yet sensing neither their own complicity nor their involvement. With a shrug, modern men and women say, "What is that to us?"

Humanity not only has vilified Judas Iscariot but has attached to all treacherous people the label Judas, thereby effectively ostracizing them from the normal flow of that portion of society in which they find themselves. Almost everyone shies away from persons who have been so identified, and since there is said to be honor even among thieves, hardened criminals handle brutally any man who has been thus tagged.

There are many undesirable qualities in all members of the human race, to greater or lesser degree, including blasphemy, deceit, doubt, denial, and a tendency to theft—to name but a few. The seeds of these traits seem to be latent within human nature, and eventually man will have to transmute them into their higher correspondences. Expressed in another way, they represent the unattainment of certain positive principles: i.e., blasphemy is the absence of right speech; deceit, the lack of honesty; doubt, a deficiency of faith or knowledge; denial, the need for affirmation; and theft, the undevelopment of shar-

---

[2] The Old Testament passage to which Jesus refers may be found in Psalms (41:9) and reads: "Yea, mine own familiar friend, in whom I trusted, which did eat of my bread, hath lifted up his heel against me."

ing. Considered in this way, betrayal is the unevolvement of loyalty or trust.

Each of the Twelve Apostles, while embodying all human qualities, undoubtedly symbolized the presence or absence of at least one positive character trait basic to discipleship. For example, John personified love, the lack of which is hate; Thomas typified doubt, which signifies inability to recognize truth; Peter exemplified denial, which is the opposite of affirmation; Judas Iscariot portrayed betrayal, which is the negative polarity to loyalty. Since little is said about the other eight apostles, no further comparisons may be drawn.

Of the undesirable qualities evinced by Thomas, Peter, and Judas, obviously the most serious is betrayal, because it is more inclusive and more insidious. ("Insidious" means not only cunning but also imperceptible, harmful progression, as in "an insidious disease.")

In one sense Thomas was rebuked by Jesus for his doubt, but there is no mention of his having been barred from the inner group as a consequence of having doubted. And Peter, who had denied the Master not once but three times, was not cast out. People explain this by pointing out that when Peter "wept bitterly," he regretted his weakness and was filled with repentance, hence could be forgiven. But if that were so, then why presumably was there no forgiveness of Judas? For he too repented, according to Matthew (27:3): "Then *Judas*, which had betrayed him, when he saw that he was condemned, *repented himself*. . . ." The obvious answer to this question is that there was no time for him to have been forgiven, inasmuch as he "went and hanged himself" as soon as he had returned the money. However, the feeling of repentance in Judas must have run deep indeed for him to commit suicide, as related in Matthew. But such a life-ending happens to dramatize vividly the self-destructive aspect of betrayal.

The tendency to betray may be likened to a viper hidden within the depths of human nature. At first it might be very small, manifesting in forms of gossip wherein personal confidences unwittingly are revealed. Gradually it could grow into a serpent of deliberate violation of trust. And as the developing personality is placed under increasing choices and tests, this snake may transform itself into a veritable dragon of self-destruction. For betrayal includes other negative factors. In order consciously to betray, a person must have certain doubts; he must deny certain things; he must lack a certain amount of love; he must practice a certain amount of deceit; and so forth. Often betrayal is not recognized until it either reaches sizable proportions or erupts under pressure.

No one knows exactly how he would act if he were physically tortured to reveal secret information or if threat were made regarding the safety of his family or military companions. Under the hammer of excruciating pain or fear of death, a person could lash out at anyone or blurt out anything. No two persons are identical, having exactly the same sense of duty or responsibility about the same values. What is important to one individual may be of little or no consequence to another. Hence one man may feel keenly that he has betrayed a trust; another under similar circumstances honestly may believe that he has acted rightly; while a third may rationalize his behavior to a point where he has convinced himself that he has done no wrong.

Further, the threshold (or breaking point) beyond which pain cannot be endured, differs in various people and is dependent to great extent upon the strength of a man's ideals and his will to live up to them.

When placed in a position of having to defend himself, the human being who has little contact or integration with his own soul might use any weapon—not only to escape physical conflict, pain, or death but to preserve an achieved position, to further an immediate goal, or even merely to avoid an unpleasant situation.

According to accepted current usage, the word "betray" implies disloyalty, treachery, or the giving of secret information to an enemy.

There are all sorts of betrayal patterns: treachery against a friend with whom one has shared bread (as the Bible points out); against members of one's household (as sometimes happened in Germany under Hitler and as occurs today in marital triangles); against one's employer, one's associates, one's country. This last form is so serious that the death penalty is imposed.

But is not the worst kind of betrayal that against one's self? Other forms may be unrecognized as such by the betrayer at the time they are committed, because of either ignorance or lack of development of higher values. But when a person *knows* beforehand that he is contemplating a traitorous act and does so anyway, he is violating his conscience and is betraying his higher self. And does this not, in very truth, constitute betrayal of the Christ principle which dwells in every man?

Until human beings can see in themselves this self-destructive quality—this composite of various negative traits—and transmute it, it could be that opportunities for other kinds of advancement in consciousness will grind almost to a halt.

Outer or objective types of treachery are bad enough; they result in the ruin of the personality in relation to society. The inner or subjective form of betrayal is incalculably worse. Remember the question that Jesus asked (Mark 8:36): ". . . what shall it profit a man if he shall gain the whole world, and lose his own soul?"

Is it not conceivable that—because of humanity's need to recognize and remove this self-destroying stumbling block from its spiritual path—betrayal *had* to be dramatized in such a way that it would be impressed indelibly upon the minds and hearts of men? If so, that portion of the Plan was enacted by Judas Iscariot.

For nearly two thousand years mankind has focused upon the reported treachery of Judas until finally a sizable percentage of men has become aware of the undesirability of this trait in its objective forms.

When humanity shall have become equally cognizant of the devastation wrought within both the individual and the race by the subjective aspect of betrayal, then the act of Judas Iscariot will have served its purpose fully.

CHAPTER 7

An Ancient Parallel

Truth is one; sages call it by various names.
                                        —*Rig-Veda* I, clxiv, 46

How MANY persons investigate, or even will listen to statements about, any faith other than that which they personally profess? Many people are incredulous—to the point of open disbelief—when told of the most elementary tenets of world religions other than their own. Since they are laboring under the illusion that their particular type of religion is unique (as indeed some of its aspects may be), they do not want to hear (for example) that the pristine teachings of the Lord Buddha are in many points identical with, and in no place contradictory of, those of the Lord Christ. As used herein, "pristine teachings" refer to those sayings that are purported to be direct quotations of the words of a religion's founder, and not to later dogma or theological interpretation.

It is perhaps safe to contend that the majority of worshippers and a goodly portion of clergy appear totally unaware that throughout the ages there has been a "continuity of revelation" —a connecting thread or chain of truth—upon which the beads of all religions are strung. It might be postulated further that from the same thread are suspended the beads of all of the knowledge in the world, not only that of religion. From the self-same chain dangle diamonds of philosophy, mathematics, science, the arts, government, social relations, economics, and so forth.

If—as is generally stated—there is but one God, then many are His faces. For if there is but one God, then behind all outer seeming there is but One Truth. Therefore it would follow that each major religion, each branch of science, each subject in every field of knowledge, is but a partial aspect of it.

There is a delightful story (credited to Gautama the Buddha, *Udana* IV, 6) about the blind men and the elephant, which may serve to illustrate this point. It runs something like this:

Once upon a time there was a certain rajah who instructed someone to gather together all of the men in that region who were born blind, and then to show them an elephant. When the blind men were assembled, to one was presented the head of the animal, to another its ear, to a third one of the tusks, to yet others the trunk, a foot, the back, the tail, and the tuft of the tail. Each was told that the portion he was given to examine was the elephant. When the rajah asked the men, "What sort of thing is an elephant?" he received various answers.

The man who had been presented with only the head said that the animal was like a pot. He who had handled the ear stated that it was similar to a winnowing basket. The fellow who had run his fingers over the tusk likened the elephant to a plowshare. The man who knew only the trunk said that it was a plow. The chap who had explored the side of the body thought of it as a granary. He who had access only to the foot was reminded of a pillar. The man on its back was convinced that it resembled a mortar. The one who had hold of the tail thought of a pestle. And to him who had been examining the tuft of the tail, the elephant was like a broom.

All of them fell to arguing heatedly until they came to blows. Each had had some personal contact and experience with the animal; therefore each was positive of the rightness of his opinion. The Buddha is said to have used this tale to emphasize that men are by nature quarrelsome and disputatious because of their ignorance of the great Law.

Substitute for the elephant the concept of the One Truth and it will be found that humanity is far more divided in conviction than were the blind men of this story.

But in either case, is it not a vision of the whole which is lacking?

Years ago there was a very human teacher who wore a ring that contained a large, sparkling, emerald-cut gem. This teacher often referred to the ring in this manner:

> Imagine, if you will, millions of infinitesimally small lives residing on all surfaces of this stone. Let us say that on one of its planes live all who follow the directions of a given religious leader; on another, individuals who believe in the instructions of the founder of a second world faith; on a third surface, perhaps those who worship Jehovah; on a fourth, followers of the Buddha; on a fifth, believers in the teaching of the Christ; on a sixth, all Moslems, et cetera.
>
> Now since all of these lives are relatively so microsopic, their sight so limited, and their capacity to visualize so undeveloped, each is certain—beyond any shadow of doubt—that the plane on which he lives, or the teaching upon which he attempts to base his life, represents the entire Truth. However, it is not until such lives are capable of rising above it in consciousness that they can perceive all facets as constituting one precious stone and eventually come to realize that even the entire jewel is not Truth itself, but merely one of the physical means whereby the light of Truth is refracted and reflected.

The two major characters to be presented in this chapter exemplify but another, earlier facet of the One Truth. The religion built around them is as a bead strung long ago on the single chain of revelation. Its size, color, shape, and material composition may appear to differ radically from modern beads, but running through its core is the same thread or chain that connects them all.

If a true inquirer were to peel off the masks of manmade dogma and ritual, strip away the outer trappings designed to facilitate devotion and donation, and allow for differences in symbol and language, culture and time, it might be discovered that there is indeed a "continuity of revelation" in process of gradual unfoldment.

Unquestionably there are many allegories from the religions of the Far East that could have been used as well to stress certain concepts in this work, but perhaps none would prove more interesting to most Christians than the story of Osiris and Set. One wonders how many of those who profess the Christ are aware that three thousand five hundred years before He was born—or about five thousand five hundred years ago—there was in the world a religion of resurrection.

In his comprehensive study entitled *Osiris, the Egyptian Religion of Resurrection*, first published in two volumes in 1911, Dr. E. A. Wallis Budge of the British Museum has made a major contribution to revolutionizing thought concerning the origin and development of ancient religions. A complete reproduction of the original text (but bound as one book and with a reduction in plate size of a few of its many illustrations) was published in 1961 (University Books, Inc., New Hyde Park, New York). Excerpts in this chapter are taken from the 1961 edition, with permission to quote having been kindly granted by the publishers.

As to the time span, the Preface of this volume is most clear: "Other dogmas made Osiris to suffer death at the hands of Set, to beget a son by Isis after his death, to rise from the dead in a transformed body, and to dwell in heaven as the lord of righteous souls. This information is derived from texts which are as old as the VIth dynasty, and thus we see that as early as 3500 B.C. the Egyptians believed that gods became incarnate in man."[3]

In this Preface, Dr. Budge also states: "The central figure of the ancient Egyptian Religion was Osiris, and the chief fundamentals of his cult were the belief in his divinity, death, resurrection, and absolute control of the destinies of the bodies and souls of men. The central point of each Osirian's Religion was his hope of resurrection in a transformed body and of immortality, which could only be realized by him through the death and resurrection of Osiris."[4]

A marked similarity to Jesus is immediately apparent. Dr.

---

[3] E. A. Wallis Budge, *Osiris, the Egyptian Religion of Resurrection* (New Hyde Park, N.Y.: University Books, Inc., 1961), Preface p. xxix.
   [4] *Ibid.*, p. xi.

Budge, however, declares that it is wrong to class the religion
of ancient Egypt with either Asiatic or European religions having elaborate theological systems or to attempt to discover in it
comparisons with the theological thought of peoples on higher
levels of civilization.

Bearing his warning in mind and allowing for differences in
time, location, tradition, and custom, a further portion of the
Preface reads:

> Of the Egyptian works mentioned above the most important for
> the purpose of an enquiry into the Religion of Ancient Egypt is
> the Book "Per-em-hru," commonly known as the Book of the
> Dead. In the oldest form of it with which we are acquainted,
> namely, that which was in use under the Vth and VIth dynasties,
> it consists of a long series of spells, and incantations, and rhy-
> thmical formulae, etc., which were recited by the priests, probably
> at regular intervals during the year, for the benefit of the dead.
> . . . Mixed with these spells are short texts which show that so
> far back as 3400 B.C. the Egyptians possessed conceptions of
> truth, justice, and righteousness. According to these the life
> everlasting in heaven, in the kingdom of Osiris, could only be
> attained by those who had lived righteous lives upon earth, and
> who had been declared to be speakers of the truth in the Judg-
> ment Hall of Osiris.[5]

Note that the primitive Egyptians here are credited with
definite concepts of truth, justice, and righteousness. It is said
that they placed the speaking of truth above all other virtues
and that Osiris himself was declared by the gods to be "Truth-
Speaker."

Osiris, the divine ancestor of the ancient Egyptians, was the
symbol of their hope of resurrection and immortality. In his
divine nature he had power to help people in the dense physical
world and in the hereafter. But it was his human nature that
enabled him to understand their needs, troubles, and griefs and
gave him the faculty of sympathy and compassion, for he—like
Jesus—had lived in a mortal body, had suffered, and had died.

---

[5] *Ibid.*, pp. xiv, xv.

It is related: ". . . for all there was only the same hope, and that hope was Osiris. Osiris the god became this hope because he had lived in a body which had suffered, and died, and had been mutilated, and had, after reconstitution, been raised from the dead by the god incarnate in it, and had passed into heaven."[6]

Now, Osiris did not undergo crucifixion as did Jesus. But legend has it that he most definitely was betrayed and killed. Later his betrayer hacked the remains into fourteen pieces (some classical writers say twenty-six) and scattered them all over Egypt. Osiris' wife, Isis, searched for and found all of the pieces except one, after which she rejoined them with wax and aromatic spices and entrusted the reconstituted body to the priests for burial.

Many persons, having a smattering of knowledge about Egypt, believe implicitly that the religion of Osiris was polytheistic because of the reverence paid to various "gods" in the forms of crocodiles, frogs, beetles, bulls, etc., as depicted in paintings and recorded by hieroglyphics on the walls of monuments and tombs. But such has been proved to be a misconception, for it is stated:

> The Recensions of the Book of the Dead and cognate works prove that, in addition to Osiris, the Egyptians paid divine honours to the Sun-god, Moon-god, Air-god, Water-god, Sky-god, Earth-god, Nile-god, and to a host of spirits, of whom we know the names of about three thousand. What relation all these "gods" and spirits bore to each other and to Osiris, is not at first clear, and it is the realization of the existence of these which has induced some writers to declare that the Egyptian Religion was nothing but a polytheistic cult. And yet it was not, for the Egyptians believed in the existence of One Great God, self-produced, self-existent, almighty and eternal, Who created the "gods," the heavens and the sun, moon and stars in them, and the earth and everything on it, including man and beast, bird, fish, and reptile. They believed that He maintained in being everything which He had created, and that He was the support

---

[6] *Ibid.*, p. xxv.

88 *Judas Iscariot*

of the universe and the Lord of it all. Of this God they never attempted to make any figure, form, likeness, or similitude, for they thought that no man could depict or describe Him, and that all His attributes were quite beyond man's comprehension. On the rare occasions in which He is mentioned in their writings He is always called "Neter" [hieroglyph], i.e., God, and besides this He has no name.[7]

The history of Osiris is told somewhat differently by such various classical writers as Herodotus, Diodorus, Plutarch, and Apuleius, probably because at the time that they wrote, Egyptian hieroglyphics had not yet been deciphered and of necessity their stories were based upon what they were told by Egyptian priests or by their educated friends who had traveled in Egypt.

It is said that much of the work of these classical authors contains valuable data, part of which has been found to be supported by native Egyptian texts. However, there was also much that is contradicted by statements shown on ancient monuments.

From the writings of Plutarch, who was born about the middle of the first century after Christ, comes one version of the story of Osiris. According to Plutarch, Osiris was born of the Sky-goddess Nut and the Earth-god Keb. After he became king, Osiris is said to have improved greatly the condition of his subjects by changing their barbarous manners, teaching them agriculture, and formulating for them a code of laws. He instructed them also to worship and serve the gods, after which he departed from Egypt and traveled widely, teaching similar lessons to men everywhere he went. In his absence his kingdom was administered by his wife, Isis, who reportedly also had great wisdom.

However, Osiris had a brother—known variously as Set, Suti, Theba, and Typhon—who surely must have been one of the earliest historical archetypes or models upon which betrayal was patterned, if the following story from Plutarch has any basis in fact (the Greek word Typhon being used in place of the Egyptian name Set):

---

[7] *Ibid.*, pp. xxvii, xxviii.

After Osiris returned from his travels Typhon appears to have made up his mind to get rid of him, and to seize the kingdom, and to take possession of his wife, Isis, with whom he was violently in love. With the view of carrying out his baleful design, he hatched a plot, and persuaded seventy-two persons, as well as a certain queen of Ethiopia, who was called Aso . . . , to join in the conspiracy. He caused a very handsome box, or chest, to be made the exact size of the body of Osiris, the measure of which he had caused to be taken by craft, and having richly decorated it, he had it brought into his dining room and left there. He then invited Osiris to a banquet, at which all the fellow-conspirators were present, and whilst the guests were admiring the handsome box, Typhon, speaking as if in jest, declared that he would give it to him that was able to lie down comfortably in it. Thereupon one after the other of the seventy-two conspirators tried to get into the box, but were unable to do so. At length Osiris expressed his willingness to make trial if the box would contain him, and finding that it did he lay down in it. All the conspirators rushed to the box, and dragging the cover quickly over it, they fastened it in position with nails, and then poured lead over it. Thus it became impossible for Osiris to breathe, and he was suffocated. The conspirators, under the direction of Typhon, then dragged the box from the banqueting hall to the bank of the Nile, and cast it into the river, which carried it northwards, and it passed out to sea by the Tanitic mouth of the Nile. The day of the murder of Osiris was the 17th of the month of Hathor [November], when the sun was in the constellation of Scorpio; according to some Osiris was in the 28th year of his reign, and according to others, in the 28th year of his age.[8]

Here is a villain of the first order. To Typhon is attributed a personal or selfish motive, about which there can be no mystery or doubt. He himself "hatched a plot" involving seventy-two persons, including a queen. Elsewhere in the book, *Osiris,* it is stated that Set (or Typhon) gave to each of the conspirators a piece of the mutilated corpse to serve as a reminder of their involvement and equal guilt, in order that they should help him obtain the throne of Osiris and defend him after he had done so.

Set not only caused a special chest to be made and arranged

---

[8] *Ibid.,* I, 2–4.

an elaborate banquet, but devised a sort of game to trap his brother and so suffocate him. And it was not enough that he had the box dragged to the river and cast therein but later, when Osiris' body finally was recovered by Isis and temporarily hidden, Set found it, cut it to pieces, and scattered the fragments over a wide area.

This is betrayal by one who apparently was a master of betrayal. The fact that Set was not just a friend of Osiris, with whom he had shared bread, but a blood brother, somehow makes his scheming and actions doubly despicable.

To quote again:

> Osiris suffered death because he was righteous, and because he had done good to all men. Osiris, being the son of a god, knew well the wickedness which was in Set, and the hatred which the personification of evil and his fiends bore to him, yet he did not seek to evade his murderous attack, but willingly met his death. There is nothing in the texts which justifies the assumption that Osiris knew that he would rise from the dead, and that he would become the king and judge of the dead, or that the Egyptians believed that Osiris died on their behalf and rose again in order that they also might rise from the dead. But from first to last the resurrection of Osiris is the great and distinguishing feature of the Egyptian religion, for Osiris was the firstfruits of the dead, and every worshipper of Osiris based his own hope of resurrection and immortality upon the fundamental fact of the resurrection of Osiris.[9]

Observe that it is said specifically that there is nothing in the ancient texts to justify any assumption that Osiris knew in advance that he would rise from the dead, that he would become judge of the dead, or that the Egyptians believed that he had "died on their behalf and rose again in order that they also might rise from the dead." Note also, however, that being the son of a god, he is said to have known the wickedness which was in Set, but did not seek to evade the murderous attack and will-

---

[9] *Ibid.*, pp. 312, 313.

ingly met his death. Jesus likewise knew about His forthcoming betrayal and death. Nor did He seek to evade His destiny. And He too has been referred to as the "firstfruits" of those who slept.

What, in that dim past, was the fate of betrayers? What happened to a person considered guilty of treason? In ancient Egypt the "other world" or the "hereafter" was known as the Ṭuat. Of this region Osiris became the overlord.

It is written:

> And thus it was with Osiris, Overlord of the Tuat. Every soul in his kingdom belonged to him absolutely and drew its means of support from him. In the Book Âm-Ṭuat we see the god seated on his throne watching the slaughter of those who have rebelled against him; their limbs are fettered, and then they are dragged into the presence of the god and their heads cut off. Treason to the mind of the African king is the gravest of all offenses, and is always punished by death, which is usually accompanied by tortures, and thus was treason punished in the Ṭuat. The headsman of Osiris and his assistants in the Ṭuat were as busily occupied as are the executioners in the service of African kings at the present day.[10]

It is especially noteworthy that treason 5,500 years ago possibly was considered "the gravest of all offenses." Perhaps it has been so considered throughout the ages. If this is true, and in view of the tendency to treason existing in the world, it may have been deemed essential that betrayal be vividly reenacted during the time of Christ. Again the drama of two basic principles—two opposing forces, two polarities—portrayed by two exemplars.

Of particular interest in a study of the religion of Osiris is the sharp delineation between light and darkness. Osiris was believed to be the embodiment of good, and Set the personification of evil. Corresponding contrasts are encountered in Christianity thirty-five centuries later but, as it were, on a

---

[10] *Ibid.,* II, 163, first printed in London in 1911.

higher turn of the spiral. While it is true that definite similarities are to be found in the stories concerning Osiris and Jesus, there also are decided differences. The same could be said about Set and Judas Iscariot, but in their case the differences might be considered greater—in number, in kind, and in degree.

When carefully studied and compared by an unbiased mind —after allowance is made for allegory, myth, legend, and additional revelation of the One Truth—may it not be admitted that certain basic teachings are common to both resurrection religions?

There is, however, something strange and apparently contradictory in these early tales. For when the body of Osiris was reassembled and ready to leave for heaven, some difficulty was encountered and it was found necessary to use a ladder to raise him to the sky; whereupon one legend has it that Horus and Set (the betrayer) procured the ladder and assisted Osiris to ascend and enter into heaven. An unusual service indeed for a betrayer, if the story is read literally. But may there not be some metaphysical or mystical symbolism involved?

According to Dr. Budge:

> The dismemberment of the body [of Osiris] was the work of a god called Set, who, curiously enough, appears at one time to be a friend of the dead man, and at another to be his bitter foe. Thus, in one place, Set and Thoth are called his two brothers, and they are mentioned in connection with Isis and Nephthys who weep for him. In another, Set is called upon to give life to Osiris and to make him live. . . . On the other hand we have in the text . . . definite statements that Set is the arch-enemy of Osiris.[11]

And so it appears at the end of the story that Set, the ancient Egyptian prototype of evil—past master in methods of betrayal— turns out to be as much as, or even more of, a mystery and an enigma to modern scholars as does Judas Iscariot, who lived 3,500 years later.

---

[11] *Ibid.*, I, 81

CHAPTER 8

Polarity

Satan represents metaphysically simply the reverse or the polar opposite of everything in Nature. He is the "Adversary," allegorically, the "Murderer," and the great Enemy of all, because there is nothing in the whole Universe that has not two sides—the reverses of the same medal.
H. P. BLAVATSKY,   *The Secret Doctrine* (Vol. 11, pp. 406, 407)

SINCE IT has been predicated in an earlier chapter that Judas Iscariot may have portrayed the role of polar opposite to Jesus, much as Satan is said to be the polar opposite of God, perhaps it would be well to examine the concept of polarity and to say a few words about Satan.

Various dictionaries define, in part, the word "polarity" as the quality of having two opposite poles (as in a magnet) or as the condition of being attracted to one pole and repelled by the other. In such case the attracting pole would be termed positive and the repelling pole negative.

In the manifested universe—in order that the universe *be* manifest—there are two basic opposing polarities or principles, which men call by different names. For example, there is spirit (positive pristine energy) and matter (negative primordial substance), the interplay between or fusion of which produces a third aspect that might be called consciousness. Expressed in different terminology: the active Father (or spirit) when wedded with the passive Mother (matter) eventuates in the Son (or soul). Yet another wording might be: Life and Appearance result in Quality (or the cosmic Christ principle incarnate in form).

For greater ease of comprehension, consider the plug of any ordinary appliance cord and the wall outlet into which it is to be fitted. In most residential areas the voltage is such that the plug will have two prongs, and the wall outlet two corresponding slits. If either prong is missing, no current will pass through the cord after the plug has been inserted into the outlet. It makes no difference which prong is lacking, for both poles—positive *and negative*—are required for the transmission of electricity. Should a third prong be present, its purpose is to provide the safety factor of a ground for higher voltages. The point to be emphasized is that two opposing polarities—positive and negative—are necessary in order that a third aspect or condition can be produced.

A few additional suggestions of common polarities and some possible effects of their interrelationships are tabulated below:

Positive Polarity	Negative Polarity	Possible Effect
male	female	offspring
pleasure	pain	self-consciousness
day	night	sense of time
birth	death	awareness of cycles
desire	object	concrete knowledge
knowledge	ignorance	development of intellect
good	evil	unfoldment of conscience
trust	betrayal	personal responsibility
peace	war	harmony through conflict
beauty	ugliness	growth of artistic sense
heart	mind	love/wisdom
order	chaos	gradual realization of, and service to, cosmic laws

Like magnetic poles are said to repel each other, while unlike poles (positive and negative) attract. Therefore spirit and matter, being of opposite polarities, are attracted to one another. The space around a magnet—for as far out as the magnet's force acts—is called a magnetic field. Such a field is invisible but may be demonstrated by a simple experiment: after sprinkling iron filings on a sheet of cardboard or glass, holding the sheet over a bar magnet, and tapping it gently, one notices that the filings arrange themselves in curved lines of force between the two magnetic poles. Such force-lines surround the magnet and constitute its magnetic field.

Similarly every manifested body (including that of man) is enclosed within its own magnetic field because of the fact that it has both positive and negative polarity. This is equally true of every group, every cell, every molecule, and every atom. And since for unknown thousands of years human beings have observed diametrically opposed forces in nature, perhaps it was inevitable that the positive spirit or life energy eventually would be termed good, or God, and the negative, material, counterbalancing force finally would come to be referred to as evil, or Satan.

Not only every temptation, test, and obstacle but every destructive, disintegrating, decaying action is attributed by Christians generally to the devil, or Satan. Christian theology has gone through strenuous mental and verbal gymnastics in endeavoring to explain how it is that Satan has such power and why God permits such an evil being to exist and to oppose Him. In this regard it is most interesting to recall the three aspects of the Hindu trinity: i.e., Brahma, the creator; Vishnu, the preserver; Shiva, the destroyer. With the Hindus, destruction is one of the aspects of God; it is not assigned to a separate entity.

It is difficult to imagine what the world would be like without the beneficent destroying action which breaks down and returns the matter of damaged, crystallized, or worn-out forms to the reservoir of basic substance whence it came. Try to conceive of the planet without such a disintegrating force. Millions upon uncounted millions of corpses—vegetable, animal, and human— vacated by the life and consciousness that had animated and informed them, would be piled miles high all over the land surface of the globe as well as on the bottoms of seas and oceans. It is unthinkable.

Some slight idea of the number of dead human bodies there might be is suggested by the following statement from *Osiris, the Egyptian Religion of Resurrection,* by E. A. Wallis Budge:

"If we assume that during the Dynastic Period, which lasted about four thousand years, the population of Egypt was about four million, and that the average duration of a generation was twenty-five years, we find that the number of bodies to be disposed of would reach the large total of *eight hundred millions.*"[12]

Such an estimate, if extended to cover the population of the entire planet both prior to and subsequent to the Egyptian dynastic period, would reach almost astronomical proportions. And this refers only to human corpses.

Is not decay or disintegration of such forms as much a divine activity as are their creation and temporary preservation? How else could life and consciousness—or spirit and soul—redeem matter or raise it in quality, unless inadequate forms were shattered and the basic substance (out of which they were made) reworked to provide more suitable, more highly refined vehicles? How better to embody the inflow of such powerful, expanding energies?

There is a Law of Economy in nature wherein nothing is wasted. Everything is used in what wisely has been referred to by a great Teacher as a "divine circulatory flow." In this sense nothing is ever destroyed. It is reworked, recombined, or reformed, as the case may be.

The smallest particle of matter, when violently bombarded, has been found to release incredible amounts of energy. If it is true that matter is crystallized energy, then someday the reverse might be demonstrated by men of science; i.e., energy, properly condensed or compressed, may assume atomic form.

Aside and apart from the obvious examples of the circulatory and respiratory systems in human and certain animal bodies, there is a planetary circulation of water. Rain falls from the sky, refreshes the life on the planet, and finds its way eventually to rivers and thence to the sea. Water evaporates or changes to a vapor where temperatures permit. Hot, dry air, in passing over

---

[12] E. A. Wallis Budge, *Osiris the Egyptian Religion of Resurrection* (New Hyde Park, N.Y.: University Books, Inc., 1961), Preface, p. xxiv. [Italics are mine. H.B.D.]

water surfaces, gradually becomes saturated. When it is super-saturated or when there is a lowering of temperature, water vapor condenses and precipitates. Snow, hail, sleet, or rain again fall from the sky. In this way there is a perpetual planetary circulatory flow of water, in perfect balance.

Another illustration might be cited: the human and animal kingdoms require a certain percentage of oxygen to sustain life. Oxygen is a waste product of the vegetable kingdom. The vegetable kingdom, in turn, must have a certain amount of carbon dioxide for the process of photosynthesis. Carbon dioxide is one of the waste products of the human and animal kingdoms. Again, an interchange in complete (even if unconscious) harmony and equilibrium—unless violated by men.

No one will deny these examples. The physical laws upon which they are based are taught to children in the sixth and seventh grades. But what seldom if ever are taught are the concepts that there exists a perpetual planetary circulatory flow or exchange of all matter (substance), all forces, and all energies; that this complex interaction is maintained in a state of perfect balance; and that creation, preservation, and *disintegration* of forms are all equally divine.

And if it is true that the forms in all kingdoms of nature must have two polarities—positive and negative—in order to manifest, then certainly the forms in the fourth or human kingdom would constitute no exception. According to *The Secret Doctrine:*

> In human nature, evil denotes only the polarity of Matter and Spirit, a "struggle for life" between the two manifested Principles in Space and Time, which Principles are one *per se*, inasmuch as they are rooted in the Absolute. In Cosmos, the equilibrium must be preserved. The operations of the two contraries produce harmony, like the centripetal and centrifugal forces, which, being mutually inter-dependent, are necessary to each other, "in order that both should live." If one should be arrested, the action of the other would become immediately self-destructive.[13]

---

[13] H. P. Blavatsky, *The Secret Doctrine,* 3d ed. (London: Theosophical Publishing House London Ltd., 1928), I, 448.

A generous portion of humanity, apparently not recognizing the one Absolute as having potential polarity, has anthropomorphized not only the positive principle (spirit) but also the negative (matter).

Bearing this thought in mind and remembering that a modern dictionary does not create meanings for words but merely reflects or records usage, it is interesting to examine the term "Satan."

Some dictionaries say that Satan is the scriptural name representing the evil power which opposes God, but which finally is subject to God's will. In *The Random House Dictionary of the English Language,* 1966 edition, Satan is defined as "the chief evil spirit; the great adversary of man; the devil."[14]

Excerpts from the definition of the word "devil," as set forth in *An Encyclopaedia of Occultism* by Lewis Spence, are given below:

> The Hebrew conception of Satan, it is thought, arose in the post-exilic period, and exhibits traces of Babylonian or Assyrian influence. It is not likely that before the captivity any specific doctrine respecting evil spirits was held by the Hebrews. Writing on this subject, Mr. F. T. Hall in his book *The Pedigree of the Devil* says:—
>
> "The term 'Satan' and 'Satans' which occur in the Old Testament, are certainly not applicable to the modern conception of Satan as a spirit of evil. . . .
>
> "The original idea of a 'Satan' is that of an 'adversary,' or agent of 'opposition,' . . . In the Book of Job, Satan appears with a distinct personality, and is associated with the sons of God, and in attendance with them before the throne of Jehovah. He is the cynical critic of Job's actions, and in that character he accuses him of insincerity and instability; and receives permission from Jehovah to test the justice of this accusation, by afflicting Job in everything he holds dear. We have here the spy, the informer, the public prosecutor, the executioner; all embodied in Satan, the adversary: these attributes are not amiable ones but the writer does not suggest the absolute antagonism between Jehovah and Satan, which is a fundamental dogma of modern Christianity. . . ."

---

[14] *The Random House Dictionary of the English Language,* 1966 unabridged (New York, Random House, Inc.), p. 1270.

According to the orthodox Christian belief of the present day, Satan has been endowed with great powers for the purpose of tempting man to prove his fortitude. . . .[15]

There is an esoteric teaching to the effect that at one time Satan (said to be a corruption of the word Saturn) was considered as the magistrate of justice, for to him were committed weight, measure, and number. Even as Michael is believed to lead the hosts of heaven, so Satan was deemed the leader of the army of God in the abyss, which is naught but the manifested world. Both Michael and Satan once were thought of as ministers of the Father, fulfilling the divine Word. Satan was conceived of as the shadow, or as the Lord in the manifested world.

Today, many Western Christians believe that Satan is the antipode, as it were, of God.

In the previous chapter it was shown that 3,500 years *before* Christ (or almost 5,500 years ago), Osiris was the positive and Typhon (or Set) the negative polarity in the ancient religion of Egypt. Almost 2,000 years ago, when Jesus lived and taught and fulfilled His mission in Palestine, Judas Iscariot represented the negative principle in the drama of redemption.

This very general treatment of polarity would be remiss indeed if it were concluded without the following reference to the subject from the angle of esoteric philosophy. In Volume II of *The Secret Doctrine*, H. P. Blavatsky has this to say:

. . . *There is no Devil, no Evil outside mankind to produce a Devil.* Evil is a necessity in, and one of the supporters of, the Manifested Universe. It is a necessity for progress and evolution, as night is necessary for the production of day, and death for that of life—*that man may live for ever.*

Satan represents metaphysically simply the *reverse* or the *polar opposite* of everything in Nature. He is the "Adversary," allegorically, the "Murderer," and the great Enemy of *all*, because there is nothing in the whole Universe that has not two sides—

[15] Lewis Spence, *An Encyclopaedia of Occultism* (New Hyde Park, N.Y.: University Books, Inc.), pp. 122, 123.

the reverses of the same medal. But in that case, light, goodness, beauty, etc., may be called Satan with as much propriety as the Devil, since they are the Adversaries of darkness, badness, and ugliness. And now the philosophy and the *rationale* of certain early Christian sects—called *heretical* and viewed as the abomination of the times—will become more comprehensible. We may understand how it was that the sect of Satanians came to be degraded, and were anathematized without any hope of vindication in a future day, since they kept their tenets secret. How, on the same principle, the Cainites came to be degraded, and even the [Judas] Iscariotes; the true character of the *treacherous* apostle having never been correctly presented before the tribunal of humanity.[16]

---

[16] Blavatsky, *op. cit.*, II, 406, 407. Italics as in original.

CHAPTER 9

Thus Saith a Rosicrucian

The special twelve students who represented His bodyguard and executive board . . . performed their proper duties during the hours of His suffering. . . .
—H. Spencer Lewis *The Secret Doctrines of Jesus* (p. 58)

FOR THOSE who normally may not come into contact with sources other than the Holy Bible or church-related texts, it may be helpful to present a few esoteric viewpoints or interpretations regarding the Twelfth Apostle. This chapter will set forth excerpts from two valuable books published by the Ancient Mystical Order Rosae Crucis (AMORC), whose headquarters in the Western Hemisphere are located in San Jose, California.

From the time of its appearance in 1929 *The Mystical Life of Jesus,* written by the late H. Spencer Lewis, F.R.C., Ph.D., former Imperator of the Rosicrucian Order, has caused considerable controversy among many thoughtful persons. For within its pages, in addition to previously undisclosed knowledge anent the mystery period in the life of Jesus, are to be found hitherto untold facts regarding His crucifixion and resurrection. Also discussed are His miracles, symbols, ancient mystery schools, the Essenes, various Christian sects—as well as mundane, spiritual, and cosmic laws and principles.

Regarding Judas Iscariot, Dr. Lewis says in part:

The true story of the crucifixion is recorded in a number of ancient writings, all of which are very dependable and consistent in their outline of the incidents. Even Judas left a brief outline of his connection with the affair and what he noted of it. His story merely substantiates some of the points contained in the other records. The principal and most complete outlines of the story are contained in the three manuscripts written by different scribes and preserved in the monasteries of Tibet, Egypt, and India.[17]

Later in the same chapter is another paragraph in which reference to Judas is made:

Caiaphas would appear to have been a spy for the Roman government if we are to judge by the secret reports that he made to Rome regarding the activities of Jesus. On the other hand, he may have been merely a personal enemy, for he certainly did do everything possible to keep Rome informed about Jesus and to make it difficult for Jesus to continue His work. Even though Caiaphas was an eminent leader of the Sanhedrin, he did not represent this body in the reports he made, nor in the attitude he assumed. It is even indicated that Caiaphas went so far as to present large sums of money for the purpose of procuring evidence and making sure that a warrant would be issued by Rome for the arrest and trial of Jesus. So we find in this man a greater enemy to Jesus and His work than Judas.[18]

After Dr. Lewis states that there are a number of references in ancient documents to show that an assassination of Jesus had been planned by both religious fanatics and the Roman authorities, he continues:

The story of Judas as presented in the Christian version is a garbled one, modified in order to illustrate the fact that among the followers of Jesus, as with every great leader or Avatar in the past, there was one who represented the evil forces and principles of the world, and who typified the untrustworthy element met with in all phases of life. The facts of the story are that the officials appointed to arrest Jesus realized that if they attempted to arrest Him in public while He was preaching or performing His miracles, they would have to contend with a mob situation resulting in the use of arms and force, the destruction of life

---

[17] H. Spencer Lewis, *The Mystical Life of Jesus* (San Jose, Calif.: Supreme Grand Lodge of AMORC, Inc., 1929). pp. 241, 242.

[18] *Ibid.*, pp. 253, 254.

and property, and the creation of a condition not desired by either the Roman or Jewish people. Therefore, it was decided to arrest Jesus in private, when He was outside of the city and accompanied by but a few of His followers. Someone was needed, however, who could identify Him at a distance in the white raiment which so many of the Essenes wore. Judas was willing to serve in this case for the bribe that was offered him, and in truth he did typify the element in life which the story in the Christian Bible presents.

That Jesus knew of the coming events and that treachery and false reports were about to end His career, is evidenced not only in the Christian stories but in many of the private records. The soldiers representing the Roman government followed the directions of Judas, and found Jesus in His usual environment in the Garden of Gethsemane where He was wont to hold secret consultations. . . .[19]

It is to be noted that Dr. Lewis credits the Romans with Jesus' arrest. He says further:

The original twelve Apostles of Jesus were all Gentiles and selected from among those who were living in Galilee. Perhaps it has never occurred to the average Christian student to look into the lives of the Apostles and note that all of them were living in Galilee at the time of their selection to form the private council of the Christ movement. Of the twelve, all but three, Lebbeus, Paul, and Judas, were of Aryan blood and were members of the Essene Brotherhood. Lebbeus and Judas were of the Jewish race but had adopted the Gentile religion by becoming heretics and abandoning much of the Jewish doctrines. After the passing of Judas, and others, the vacancies in the Council of twelve Apostles were filled by other Gentiles of the Essene Brotherhood selected by the Council itself.[20]

Where did the Rosicrucian Imperator procure some of the information given in *The Mystical Life of Jesus?* There are ancient outlines, as stated above, in the monasteries of Tibet, Egypt, and

---

[19] Ibid., pp. 255, 256.
[20] *Ibid.*, p. 290.

India. And also it is recorded: "Fortunately for us, some very important manuscripts have survived all of the destructive processes, and it is from these that many incidents regarding the life of Jesus have been extracted for this book."[21]

Additional discussion ensued eight years later, in 1937, when the first edition of *The Secret Doctrines of Jesus,* also written by Dr. Lewis, was published by AMORC. For this volume reveals additional information about Jesus, including His secret council meetings, in which 120 members participated; His private teachings, which were not divulged to the masses; hidden keys to the parables in the New Testament; and an explanation of the passwords, signs, and symbols of the mystery school known as the Brethren in White.

The following excerpt regarding Judas Iscariot is taken from this second book:

> Let no one think for a moment that Jesus was suddenly surprised or unexpectedly shocked by either the act of Judas in betraying Him or the secret plans that were being made for His public disgrace after a manifestly illegal trial. For weeks and months the legal Lights who could be induced or bribed into lending their assistance had been preparing the papers for such a trial as Rome had never heard of before, and such as the Jews never hoped to witness again. . . . The whole procedure that seemed to come as the sudden, stupendous climax of His life was a well-evolved drama, plotted weeks, months, years, and even centuries before in the evil consciousness of that portion of all human nature which abhors the presentation of truth, the coming of Light, the dispelling of Darkness, and the victory of Spirituality. Jesus knew in His youth, during the earliest days of His preparation for the future ministry, that it would end just as it did end. But He also knew that in a certain number of years, months, weeks, days, and hours He must accomplish the great mission of His life and not permit the grand climax to come upon Him before He was ready.[22]

---

[21] *Ibid.,* p. 248.

[22] H. Spencer Lewis, *The Secret Doctrines of Jesus* (San Jose, Calif.: Supreme Grand Lodge of AMORC, Inc., 1937), pp. 109, 110.

It may be recalled that on numerous occasions when Jesus' enemies attempted to harm Him, they could not lay their hands upon Him and that one time He walked uninjured through a crowd that was in process of trying to stone Him. Thus it is evident that, in Dr. Lewis's words, He did not allow "the grand climax to come upon Him before He was ready."

In this second volume, while speaking of the events that occured just before the crucifixion. Dr. Lewis has this to say:

It was on this occasion of His last worldly supper with them that He revealed to them again why He had been anxious for many days to have this special ceremony occur. So He proceeded to explain to them that while the officials of the country were seeking Him and trying to find His hiding place to arrest Him and falsely condemn and crucify Him, it would not be until the morning or very late that evening that one of His own supposedly loyal Apostles would betray Him.

Most of His Apostles knew also of the threats that had been made and the danger that surrounded Him and so they were not surprised at His announcement, but they were startled when He told them that one of those sitting right at the very table with Him now, and participating in this last great ceremony, would be the one to betray Him. They were so startled that they began to question Jesus as to whom it could possibly be, and they grew excited and claimed that each of them was the greatest in sincerity and loyalty or that each of them was the chosen Disciple to represent the great work in the future and therefore could not be guilty of such a crime as this. In their desire to establish their individual superiority, loyalty, and fidelity, they overlooked the significance of the fact that one of them would prove before morning that he was the least worthy to claim such a high degree of faithfulness. And Jesus argued with them and rebuked them for the manner in which they were analyzing the situation.

He finally told them that this was the occasion when He was to fulfill His former great promises to them, and that at this very moment He appointed to each of them a kingdom just as His Father in Heaven had appointed a kingdom to Him, and that by this appointment they were to eat and drink at His table in His kingdom—or in other words to be co-equal with Him in this new Kingdom of Heaven on earth, in ruling it, directing it, and establishing it for all time in the future. They, as the twelve

great Lights and leaders of the secret school guiding the scores
of other faithful pupils who had been trained daily under Him,
were to carry on His great mission in the future. . . .[23]

Again it is to be noted that Jesus is said to have appointed
a kingdom to each of the Twelve. No qualification or exception
is made concerning Judas, either in this quotation or in the
Christian Bible (Luke 22:28–30).

It is interesting that Dr. Lewis postulates not only the Twelve
Apostles of Jesus nor seventy disciples as is now generally believed but a total of one hundred twenty. This number, he
claims, constituted the secret school which the Master had
formed. And it is stated that each of the Twelve Apostles headed
—as chairman or chief advisor—a group of ten, while together
they served as members of the executive committee of this select
society. See Acts (1:15) for scriptural evidence that there were,
indeed, about one hundred twenty disciples.

Concerning the claim that Jesus gave secret or inner instruction that differed from His outer teaching, there should be
no doubt, for in Mark (4:10,11) may be found indisputable
biblical verification: "And when he was alone, they that were
about him with the twelve asked of him the parable. And he
said unto them, Unto you it is given to know the mystery of
the kingdom of God: but unto them that are without, all these
things are done in parables."

In speaking of the period just after Jesus' resurrection, Judas's
name is mentioned by Dr. Lewis in passing: "And so while they
were together, the whole hundred or more of them, with the
exception of Judas, with doors locked and windows and every
portion of the premises under careful observation and protection,
Jesus appeared in their midst."[24]

The last reference to the Twelfth Apostle in Dr. Lewis's *The
Secret Doctrines of Jesus,* has to do with a gathering of disciples
for the purpose of electing Judas's successor. It is written:

---

[23] *Ibid.,* pp. 119, 120.
[24] *Ibid.,* p. 138.

The occasion for this special meeting was the election of another Apostle to take the place of Judas who had betrayed Jesus and who had suffered the loss of his earthly life as a result of his attempt to escape from his own conscience. So we find that Peter arose in the midst of this meeting and addressed them after long prayers and supplications with the following thoughts: "It was necessary that the Holy Scripture of the past and the prophecies of our ancient days should be fulfilled as the Holy Spirit had revealed to us by the mouth of David concerning *a Judas* who was to guide the enemies to the correct place where they might find our great leader and Saviour Jesus. This terrible manifestation of treason and treachery, or disloyalty and enmity had to be fulfilled. *It was decreed that Jesus should come to His timely end through the treachery of a Judas.*[Italics are mine—H.B.D.] He had been one with us, our companion, our trusted associate, but His part had been allotted to Him in the service that we were to render individually and collectively. And so it came about that one of our companions performed the necessary but regrettable act and then with the wages of his iniquity, with the bag of gold that he received, he purchased a field. And in running through it to escape from those who might see him and recognize him, and to escape the mockery of his conscience, he ran across the field to hide and in so doing he fell and injured himself and brought death to himself, and he bled profusely upon the field even to such an extent that all who heard of it at once nicknamed the field Aceldama, which means *a field of blood.*"

"You will recall," said Peter to the assembly, "that it is written in the Book of Psalms, 'Let his habitation become desolate and let no man dwell in it: and let another take his office.' "

Then Peter explained to them that the vacancy in their midst must be filled by one who could be a witness to all of the acts of Jesus—even a witness of His Crucifixion and His Resurrection. Therefore they must choose as a successor to Judas one who had been a companion with them all the time that Jesus had been in and around and among them. So they selected two who could fill the position. . . . After more prayer in which they petitioned God, who knew the hearts of all of them to show them which of the two had been selected on high to take up the part of the ministry and Apostleship which Judas had deserted, they finally voted with ballots and the selection fell to Matthias, and he was numbered with the other eleven Apostles to make the number of twelve complete.[25]

---

[25] *Ibid.,* p. 164–66.

The attention of the reader is called to the statement that "it was decreed that Jesus should come to His timely end through the treachery of a Judas." Evidently the plan of the Spiritual Hierarchy at that time included an act of betrayal. Why? In the following sentence may be found the reason: Jesus knew that he would be betrayed and was aware, as stressed by Dr. Lewis, "that again, as in thousands of instances in the story of past civilization, one traitor must be found in the midst of the true and loyal to exemplify the spirit of darkness and the character of Satan."[26]

Perhaps there is no better way to end this chapter than by requoting the provocative thought with which it began: "The special twelve students who represented His bodyguard and executive board . . . performed their proper duties during the hours of His suffering. . . ."[27]

---

[26] *Ibid.,* p. 57
[27] *Ibid.,* p. 58.

CHAPTER 10

New Age Bible Interpretation

Judas, of the tribe of Judah (Leo), signifies the heart when linked to the lower sense life: the Christ, the supreme symbol of Leo, is this same heart power at one with the Spirit.
—New Age Bible Interpretation (Vol. IV, New Testament, Part II, p. 165)

FROM A MOST comprehensive study entitled *The New Age Bible Interpretation,* (New Age Press, Inc., Oceanside, California) is taken the material concerning Judas Iscariot for this chapter. All of the extracts are from Volume IV, which is based on the New Testament. Permission to quote was generously given by Mr. Theodore Heline, executive director. The entire series of four volumes constitutes "An Exposition of the Inner Significance of the Holy Scriptures in the Light of the Ancient Wisdom," as stated on the flyleaf.

An introduction to Judas is given in the following paragraph:

Judas Iscariot was the man of mystery, the betrayer of the Christ. He came from Kerioth, which belonged to the tribe of Judah. This tribe is governed by Leo, the heart sign, and symbolizes one in whom the love nature is linked with the sense life. Judas portrays the state of the average man who daily betrays the Christ, the Higher Self, within. Each of the twelve Disciples represents a specific faculty or attribute of man himself: *Judas, therefore, will play his role in human evolution until such time as the lower nature of the race shall be redeemed.* He destroyed himself, as all evil ultimately destroys itself, and was replaced by Matthias, the symbol of the redeemed man of the New Age and the new race.[28]

---

[28] *The New Age Bible Interpretation* (Oceanside, Calif.: New Age Press, Inc.), Vol. IV, Part II pp. 81, 82. [Italics are mine. H.B.D.]

Volume IV next sets forth the qualities and attributes of the Twelve Apostles and casts considerable light upon the significance of the number 12.

Peter is the man of action; John, the man of prayer; Thomas, the skeptic; James, the aspiring; Nathanael, the dreamer; James, the methodical; Andrew, the humble; Philip, the commonplace; Thaddeus, the courageous; Matthew, the servant of Rome; Simon, the rebel against Rome; and Judas, the betrayer.

Twelve is the most important number of the New Testament, for twelve is the perfect number of Deity in a cycle of expression. The new Holy City as portrayed in Revelation has twelve gates that are never closed. With the ending of the cycle of twelve a new manifestation of life begins on a higher round. Thus the incidents in the life of every Teacher who brings a cosmic message to humanity parallel the passage of the Sun through the twelve zodiacal signs.

There always have been twelve physical and twelve spiritual powers manifesting in humanity, corresponding to twelve spiritual centers in the body, which, when awakened, are symbolized by twelve lights, or the "flowers that bloom upon the cross." These centers are to be awakened as man progresses into higher phases of development; they represent the divine consummation of God's great plan for the entire human family at the end of the present Earth Period.

The following table correlates the Twelve Disciples with attributes of character and with the twelve signs of the Zodiac.

JAMES	Hope	Aries
ANDREW	Strength	Taurus
THOMAS	Doubt	Gemini
NATHANAEL*	Intuition	Cancer
JUDAS	Passion	Leo
JAMES (son of Alpheus)	Method	Virgo
THADDEUS	Courage	Libra
JOHN	Regeneration	Scorpio
PHILIP	Spiritual Knowledge	Sagittarius
SIMON	Enthusiasm	Capricorn
MATTHEW	Spiritual Will	Aquarius
PETER	Faith	Pisces

*[Probably Bartholomew—H.B.D.]

The twelve cosmic principles manifesting in the universe may be correlated with the Twelve Disciples thus:

1. Will	James	Hope	*The perfect Trinity:* "*Now abideth Faith, Hope, and Love. But the greatest of these is Love.*"
2. Wisdom	John	Love	
3. Activity	Peter	Faith	
4. Contraction	Thomas	Doubt	
5. Expansion	James the Less	Growth of Spirit	
6. Attraction	Andrew	Strength	
7. Repulsion	Simon	Zeal	
8. Crystallization	Matthew	Custom	
9. Construction	Thaddeus	Courage	
10. Destruction	Judas	Passion	
11. Addition or Increase	Nathanael*	Intuition—Imagination	
12. Reflection (As above, so below)	Philip	Spiritual Knowledge[29]	

Again it is pointed out that the lower or outer self, known in these days as the personality of an individual, is in conflict with the higher or inner nature, and that Judas may be considered as a symbol of unregenerate outer man on the dense physical plane: "Judas Iscariot, the lower self, always objects to the higher nature dedicating itself to the works of the Christ. 'The poor' (those who are not yet ready for this high place in the spiritual life) 'ye have always with you, but me ye have not always' (upon the earth functioning in a physical body)."[30]

After stating that John and Judas possibly were the only Apostles to escape martyrdom, the next reference to the Twelfth Apostle may be found in the section which discusses the Passion tide: "On the third day Judas succumbed to the temptation of the priests. Judas typifies the lower, instinctive nature; the

---

*[Probably Bartholomew. H.B.D.]

[29] *Ibid.,* pp. 83—85.

[30] *Ibid.,* p. 112.

priests, the human or mortal. When these two forces are paramount, the Christ or spiritual nature is always betrayed and, in turn, their own self-destruction is inevitable as instanced by Judas' tragic end."[31]

In speaking of the more esoteric meanings of the Last Supper, Volume IV says, in part, about the bread: " 'Take, eat, this is my body.' These were not mere empty words spoken as the bread was eaten. As previously stated, only those partook who were able to infuse into the elements a spiritual power and only holy men were able to do this."[32]

Among other comments concerning the wine, it is said: "Mark's account of the Last Supper states that all of the Disciples drank of it, meaning thereby that they all qualified for the deeper spiritual works."[33]

Shortly thereafter, there ensues the following fascinating passage about the betrayal: "The secret of the betrayal was known only by the Christ, Judas, Peter and John. The powers of faith and love always effect a transformation of the lower nature. 'He then having received the sop went immediately out; and it was night.' "[34]

When reading the next quotation, the reader is asked to hold in mind the fact that Judas Iscariot was present at the Last Supper during the ritual of the bread and the wine, as may be verified by reference to Luke (22:19–21) or Mark (14:16–23):

> The ceremony of the Last Supper represents the complete transmutation of the lower nature into the higher; consequently Judas, the lower, could not remain. *It is one of the twelve that dippeth with me in the dish.* The awakened Christ within works upon mortal man and uses this redeemed power in building the new golden chalice of the soul. Chapters XIV to XVII of John's Gospel contain the most profound spiritual work given the

---

[31] *Ibid.,* p. 146.
[32] *Ibid.,* p. 150
[33] *Ibid.*
[34] *Ibid.*

disciples. This work was revealed at the conclusion of the Holy Supper, *after the disappearance of Judas,* and is recorded only in John.[35]

That there exist various kinds or types of betrayal is made evident in the following comments about the three Apostles who slept while the Christ was praying in the Garden of Gethsemane just prior to His arrest:

> Christ Jesus was endeavoring to have Peter, James, and John leave their bodies and follow Him into the World of Life Spirit, there to read the heavenly records and to understand the esoteric meaning of His mission, that they might know that His great Passion and death were not the end, but only the beginning of His work. But they failed Him. They betrayed the Christ within themselves, as well as the great Master, for they were yet so engrossed in the material, still so given to disputing about the high places they should receive in the New Kingdom, that they were unable to follow Him; "they were asleep" to these high spiritual truths. Christ Jesus knew now that the path must be trod alone. Humanity must remain yet for a time in darkness as to the real meaning of His work. He must continue to be misunderstood and betrayed, even by His own best-beloved, until the very end. The Disciples never fully understood the inner meaning of His work until that blessed day of illumination which we know as Pentecost.[36]

Next is one explanation of the possible reasons for Judas's betrayal of Jesus:

> Judas had been made the treasurer of the band. His personal ambitions were thwarted by Christ Jesus' refusal to lead an army against Rome. He had expected the Master to proclaim Himself king and that he, Judas, should receive a high place among officials. As the Christ gave deeper and more spiritual truths, Judas became more hopelessly confused. Having no understanding of the deeper work, his confusions turned into baffled rage and hatred, culminating in the betrayal.

---

[35] *Ibid.*, pp. 150, 151. Italics as in original.
[36] *Ibid.*, pp. 158, 159.

The powers of Christ, of John and of Judas, all represent powers within ourselves. It is for us to transmute the force of Judas into that of John and so awaken the divinity of the Christ within. We may well ponder the axiom of the ancient Greeks: "Man, know thyself."[37]

Although the writers of the text quoted here say that "only Matthew and Luke mention the betrayal by Judas, the lower nature, which ever seeks to sell the higher, Christ within, to the priests or material power,"[38] Mark (14:10,11) also tells of the money arrangement: "And Judas Iscariot, one of the twelve, went unto the chief priests to betray him unto them. And when they heard it, they were glad, and promised to give him money. And he sought how he might conveniently betray him." The text, however, continues and gives esoteric meanings for silver and the figures 3 and 30:

> The betrayal was preceded by the Last Supper, the occasion for the highest spiritual teaching imparted by the Master.
>
> The lowest and the highest, the gamut of human accomplishment, is encompassed in one chapter of this Book of Books. Judas, of the tribe of Judah (Leo), signifies the heart when linked to the lower sense life; the Christ, the supreme symbol of Leo, is the same heart power at one with the Spirit.
>
> Matthew's is the Gospel of the Dedication. It is the only Gospel in which the thirty pieces of silver are mentioned. Silver is a feminine metal belonging to the Moon, and the number three is the complete dedication of the threefold aspect of man to evil symbolized in the character of Judas Iscariot, even as the gifts of the Three Wise Men signify the consecration of this same threefold aspect to the higher nature or the Christ. It is the divine plan that Judas, or the lower nature in man, shall eventually destroy or redeem itself and thereafter be supplanted by Matthias, the higher self. The key to this transmutation is given in Zachariah:
>
> *Zechariah 11:8, 12–15.*
>
> *Three shepherds also I cut off in one month; and my soul loathed them, and their soul abhorred me.*

---

37 *Ibid.*, p. 159.
38 *Ibid.*, pp. 164, 165.

*And I said unto them, if ye think good, give me my price; and
if not, forbear. So they weighed for my price thirty pieces of
silver.*

*And the Lord said unto me, Cast it unto the potter; a goodly
price that I was priced at of them. And I took the thirty pieces
of silver and cast them to the potter in the house of the Lord.*

*Then I cut asunder mine other staff, even bands, that I might
break the brotherhood between Judah and Israel.*

*And the Lord said unto me, Take unto thee yet the instruments
of a foolish shepherd.*

The three shepherds who are abhorred signify the threefold
aspect previously referred to when manifesting on the sense
plane. The price, thirty pieces of silver, must always be cast
in the house of the Lord (law) through the purification of the
body in regeneration. Until this transmutation has been accomplished man always bears the instruments of a foolish shepherd.[39]

From the section concerning the trials of Jesus, only sentences relevant to betrayal and to Judas have been extracted.
Of Judas's kiss, an entirely different interpretation from the
one below will be offered in a subsequent chapter.

The soldiers of the Sanhedrin approached, accompanied by Judas
who gave the traitorous kiss. The Christ met this with an infinite
compassion and love transcending anything the world has ever
known as He spoke gently to Judas and called him "friend."
Here is the perfect ideal for humanity to follow. . . .

Between the preliminary examination by Annas and the first
trial of Caiaphas, Christ Jesus witnessed His betrayal by Peter. . . .
As the Christ was being led away from the apartments of Annas
to those of Caiaphas, He heard the third denial. . . .

Between the trials by Caiaphas and Pilate, Judas threw the
thirty pieces of silver at the feet of the priests and went out and
hanged himself. Evil always destroys itself. Wrongdoing can only
bring its own reaction in greater evil. This is an immutable law
of all nature and finds a perfect correspondence in the lives of
the Disciples.[40]

---

[39] *Ibid.*, pp. 165, 166. Italics as in original.

[40] *The New Age Bible Interpretation* (Oceanside, Calif.: New Age
Press, Inc.), Vol. IV, Part II, pp. 167, 168.

In Part III of Volume IV of *The New Age Bible Interpretation* are given word-portraits of the Twelve Apostles, including this description of Judas Iscariot:

> There is a legend to the effect that in Jesus' youth a woman brought to Him her son afflicted with a devil. When this evil spirit came upon the boy he would bite any who came near him; if alone he would tear his own flesh. There were those who saw the evil spirit depart from the lad as he stood before the youthful Jesus. Grown to manhood, this boy became the Disciple known as Judas Iscariot.
>
> Judas Iscariot was short of stature, with a sharp, unpleasant visage. His eyes were filled with fierce light; his hair and beard were red. It has been said that he also was a member of the Zealots. At any rate, he was possessed of an intense and fiery patriotism. Like Simon, his thoughts were focussed on the establishment of a mundane glory, "My kingdom is not of this world" had no meaning for a mind like that of Judas Iscariot.
>
> He was shrewd, calculating and economical, so he was elected treasurer of the apostolic company. As John expressed it, "He carried the bag."
>
> The price of the Betrayal was thirty pieces of silver, twenty and ten. The priests were well versed in the Kaballa and the Tarot. The number ten in the Tarot is symbolized by the Wheel of Fate. Twenty represents Judgment. The priests expected that the *ten* and *twenty* would bring "swift Judgment of Fate."
>
> In remorse Judas committed suicide by hanging himself. The symbol of thirty in the Tarot is "The Hanged Man."
>
> Tradition still points out a tree, ragged, crooked and wind-whipped, standing alone upon a desolate and forbidding hill, as the "Tree of Judas."
>
> This Disciple hoped that by his betrayal he could force the Master to overawe His enemies by His supernatural powers. Judas visioned the establishment of a physical kingdom of great splendor with himself in a position of high authority.
>
> The agony of his remorse was twofold; first, disappointment for himself; second, realization of the enormity of his crime. This latter feeling overcame him. As he flung the accursed silver at the feet of the priests and rushed out to self-destruction, he moaned, "I have slain innocent blood."
>
> With this money the priests purchased the "field of blood" in which to inter the bodies of strangers.[41]

---

[41] *Ibid.*, Part iii, pp. 195, 196.

The following excerpts are included for the reason that they relate to the subject of polarity insofar as the Christian mysteries are concerned:

> Every Mystery Temple the world has ever seen was founded upon two mighty columns of truth representing perfect equilibrium of polarity between the masculine and feminine forces—a state which must exist before an aspirant is qualified to pass between these two columns and enter the temple. . . .
> In the Christian Mystery Temple the masculine column represents the Lord Christ. . . .
> The feminine column represents the supreme woman, Master of the world, the blessed Virgin Mary, Mother of the most holy Jesus.[42]

It has been said that "Judas, of the tribe of Judah (Leo), signifies the heart when linked to the lower sense life; the Christ, the supreme symbol of Leo, is this same heart power at one with the Spirit."[43] The heart is one of the most sacred keys to spiritual evolution of man. Judas Iscariot symbolized one state of the heart; the Christ the other.

---

[42] *Ibid.*, p. 205.
[43] *Ibid.*, Part II, p. 165.

CHAPTER 11

Some Esoteric Terms Defined

God sleeps in rocks, grows in plants, moves in animals, and thinks in man.
                                                    —*Eastern proverb*

BEFORE A NEW or different theory about Judas Iscariot can be presented properly, certain basic ideas, principles, or laws need to be simply defined. Such will be the main content of this chapter.

Almost everyone admits the existence of God. Especially is this true when a person is faced with excruciating pain, intense fear, or possible loss of life.

In the Orient, God is considered much as Krishna (the Christ principle) describes Himself to Arjuna (the world disciple, or developed form aspect) in *The Bhagavad Gita:* "Having pervaded the entire universe with a fragment of myself, I remain." Here the life principle (that which synthesizes spirit, soul, and body) is hinted at or implied.

But in the Occident, particularly among Christians, how is God conceived? Is He not thought of mainly as a Being somewhere in heaven, up in the sky, out in space, above His creation —much as a potter is separate from his wheel and from the clay which he molds into various forms? For almost twenty centuries, haven't most Christians imagined God as transcendent or higher than His creation? Such is the aspect of Him which has been emphasized, although admittedly a few words were pronounced here and there to the effect that God made the world out of His own substance, for nothing else is said to have existed prior to the Creation. In the West, the immanence of God has been discussed primarily among philosophers, intellectuals, and theologians; God Immanent has not been stressed in teaching the masses of men.

For example, how many persons do you know who consider God to be expressing a portion of Himself through them, much less through their friends or enemies, or through the animals which they happen to contact? How many people think of God as being in trees and other vegetation—or in the automobiles they drive, the objects they handle, or the ground upon which they walk? How many, if any, consider mountains or stones as living or as having consciousness? On the contrary, many Christians, including clergy, will object violently to such a "pantheistic" conception.

And yet if there is but one Absolute—if it is the interplay between spirit and matter that results in objective forms and in consciousness—then even an atom must possess not only life but a kind of awareness. It has been said that the consciousness of man is as far from that of God, in one direction, as it is from that of a stone or rock, in the other. The belief that matter is inert was exploded over Hiroshima and Nagasaki at the end of World War II. One wonders how much longer the school systems will continue to teach that the mineral kingdom is inanimate and without consciousness of any kind.

Provided scriptural verification for God's immanence be necessary, it is suggested that the reader consider these references:

PSALM 139:8: If I ascend up into heaven, thou art there: *if I make my bed in hell, behold, thou art there.*

LUKE 17:20, 21: And when he was demanded of the Pharisees, when the kingdom of God should come, he answered them and said, The kingdom of God cometh not with observation: Neither shall they say, Lo here! or lo there! for, behold, *the kingdom of God is within you.*

JOHN 1:4,9: In him was life; and the life was the light of men. . . . That was the true Light, which lighteth *every man* that cometh into the world.

II CORINTHIANS 6:16: . . . *ye are the temple of the living God;*

as God hath said, I will dwell in them, and walk in them. . . .
[Italics are mine. H.B.D.]

The transcendence of God is most beautifully expressed in
Acts 17:28: "For in him we live, and move, and have our
being . . ."

With reference to the ancient Eastern proverb that God
sleeps in rocks, grows in plants, moves in animals, and thinks
in man: "Esoteric Philosophy teaches that everything lives and
is conscious, but not that all life and consciousness are similar
to those of human or even animal beings. Life we look upon as
the One Form of Existence, manifesting in what is called Matter;
or what, incorrectly separating them, we name Spirit, Soul and
Matter in man. Matter is the Vehicle for the manifestation of
Soul on this plane of existence, and Soul is the Vehicle on a
higher plane for the manifestation of Spirit, and these three are
a Trinity synthesized by Life, which pervades them all."[44] A
more clear definition of God, transcendent and immanent, would
be difficult to find.

The same author defines matter thus: "Matter, to the Oc-
cultist, it must be remembered, is that totality of existences in
the Kosmos, which falls within any of the planes of possible
perception."[45] Note that this definition is not limited to current
human perception.

Evolution has been defined as:

The development of higher orders of animals from the lower.
Modern, or so-called *exact* science, holds but to a one-sided
physical evolution, prudently avoiding and ignoring the higher
or spiritual evolution, which would force our contemporaries to
confess the superiority of the ancient philosophers and psycho-
logists over themselves. The ancient sages, ascending to the

---

[44] H. P. Blavatsky, *The Secret Doctrine*, 3d ed. (London: Theosophical Publishing House London Ltd., 1928), I, 79, 80.
[45] *Ibid.*, p. 560.

UNKNOWABLE, made their starting-point from the first manifestation of the unseen, the unavoidable, and from a strict logical reasoning, the absolutely necessary creative Being, the Demiurgos of the universe. Evolution began with them from pure spirit, which descending lower and lower down, assumed at last a visible and comprehensible form, and became matter. Arrived at this point, they speculated in the Darwinian method, but on a far more large and comprehensive basis.[46]

It has been said that the five kingdoms in nature (namely: mineral, vegetable, animal, human, and spiritual) are created by the interplay of spirit and matter and their resultant consciousness or soul. In this process, as consciousness develops, new and more suitable forms are created for its expression. When the indwelling conscious life—moving through the so-called lower kingdoms—reaches the fourth, or human, kingdom, consciousness becomes individualized and forms are invested with self-awareness. But the action does not stop there. The immediate aim of each incarnating human unit is to reach the fifth, or spiritual, kingdom, that which Christians refer to as "the kingdom ofGod."

A very great Teacher, known as the Tibetan, has said that the entire evolutionary process, in the last analysis, is "the working out of the inter-relation between God and His world, between cause and effect and between Life and form."[47] He further states that the whole *goal* of the evolutionary process "is to shield, nurture and finally reveal the hidden spiritual reality."[48]

If these declarations are true (and who, indeed, can prove that they are not?), then in what manner or by what general method is such a goal reached?

In the East, evolution is said to be implemented by twin

---

[46] H. P. Blavatsky, *Isis Unveiled* (Pasadena, Calif.: Theosophical University Press, 1960), I, xxx, xxxi.

[47] Alice A. Bailey, *A Treatise on the Seven Rays* (New York: Lucis Publishing Company), III (Esoteric Astrology), 626.

[48] *Ibid*, pp. 251, 252.

laws—the Law of Reincarnation and the Law of Karma. Expressed in different terms, they sometimes are called the Law of Rebirth and the Law of Cause and Effect. These two basic laws (or distortions thereof) are believed in by, or are known to, millions of people. They have been taught for thousands of years.

With regard to reincarnation or rebirth, it has been written:

> The doctrines of Theosophy are simply the faithful echoes of Antiquity. Man is a *Unity* only at his origin and at his end. All the Spirits, all the Souls, gods and demons emanate from and have for their root-principle the SOUL OF THE UNIVERSE—says Porphyry (*De Sacr.*). Not a philosopher of any notoriety who did not believe (1) in reincarnation (metempsychosis), (2) in the plurality of principles in man, or that man had *two* Souls of separate and quite different natures; one perishable, the *Astral Soul,* the other incorruptible and immortal; and (3) that the former was not the man whom it represented—"neither his spirit nor his body, but his *reflection,* at best." This was taught by Brahmins, Buddhists, Hebrews, Greeks, Egyptians and Chaldeans; by the postdiluvian heirs of the prediluvian Wisdom, by Pythagoras and Socrates, Clemens Alexandrinus, Synesius and Origen, the oldest Greek poets as much as the Gnostics, whom Gibbon shows as the most refined, learned and enlightened men of all ages (see "Decline and Fall," etc.). But the rabble was the same in every age: superstitious, self-opinionated, materializing every most spiritual and noble idealistic conception and dragging it down to its own low level, and—ever adverse to philosophy.[49]

In the same work there is the following definition of metempsychosis (reincarnation):

> The progress of the soul from one stage of existence to another. Symbolized and vulgarly believed to be rebirths in animal bodies. A term generally misunderstood by every class of European and American society, including many scientists. The kabalistic axiom "A stone becomes a plant, a plant an animal, an animal a man, a man a spirit, and a spirit a god," receives an explanation in

---

[49] Blavatsky, *Isis Unveiled,* II, Appendix, A-44.

Manu's *Manava-Dharma-Sastra*, and other Brahmanical books.[50]

According to the Tibetan: "Reincarnation is implicit in the manifested universe and is a basic and fundamental theme underlying systematic pulsation."[51] In the same volume, a few pages further on, there is this explanation:

> It would appear that as yet only two rules are posited in connection with the return of an ego to physical incarnation. The first is that if perfection has not been achieved then the soul must return and continue the perfecting process upon the Earth. The second is that the impulse predisposing the ego to such action is some form of unsatisfied desire. Both these statements are true in part and generic in effect but they are only partial truths and incident to larger truths which have not yet been sensed or noted accurately by esotericists; they are secondary in nature and are expressed in terms of the three worlds of human evolution, of personality intent, and of time-space concepts. Basically, it is not desire which prompts return but will and knowledge of the plan. It is not the need for achieving an ultimate perfection which goads the ego on to experience in form, for the ego is already perfect. The main incentive is sacrifice and service to those lesser lives that are dependent upon the higher inspiration (which the spiritual soul can give) and the determination that they too may attain planetary status equivalent to that of the sacrificing soul.[52]

Of various New Testament references to the idea of rebirth or reincarnation, the following might be considered:

> MATTHEW 11:13–15: For all the prophets and the law prophesied until *John. And if ye will receive it, this is Elias,* which was for to come. He that hath ears to hear, let him hear.
> MATTHEW 17:10–13: And his disciples asked him, saying, Why then say the scribes that Elias must first come? And Jesus answered and said unto them, Elias truly shall first come, and

---

[50] *Ibid.*, I, xxxvi, xxxvii.
[51] Bailey, *op. cit.*, III, 312.
[52] *Ibid.*, p. 324.

restore all things. *But I say unto you, That Elias is come already, and they knew him not,* but have done unto him whatsoever they listed. Likewise shall also the Son of man suffer of them. *Then the disciples understood that he spake unto them of John the Baptist.*

MARK 8:27,28: "And Jesus went out, and his disciples, into the towns of Caesarea Philippi: and by the way he asked his disciples, saying unto them, *Whom do men say that I am?* And they answered, John the Baptist: but some say, Elias; and others, One of the prophets.

In reference to the Law of Reincarnation or Rebirth, it might be postulated—in a very unsatisfactory and oversimplified fashion in order to clarify the idea—that the indwelling, perpetually expanding consciousness creates, uses, and vacates countless forms during its journey back to the Father's house. Even as a man during his life wears various clothes to suit differing conditions, so the soul in its long series of lives is said to use many outer garments or bodies.

Karma has been defined as "Physical action. Metaphysically, the law of retribution; the law of cause and effect, or ethical causation. There is the karma of merit and the karma of demerit. It is the power that controls all things, the resultant of moral action, or the moral effect of an act committed for the attainment of something which gratifies a personal desire."[53]

It has been pointed out that

> . . . karma fulfills itself in relation to the form nature upon which it expends its energy and that where there is a static condition and a quiescent attitude, the process moves but slowly; the life then within the form fails to experience the needed, forceful awakening; inevitably then there lies ahead a repetition of the process until the time comes when activity and response is evoked. This then *leads to resistance to the apparent karmic necessity and this brings about liberation.* Only through resistance to evil . . . can karma be brought to an end.[54]

[53] Alice A. Bailey, *Initiation, Human and Solar* (New York: Lucis Publishing Company), p. 219.

[54] Bailey, *Treatise on Seven Rays*, III, 444. [Italics as in original.]

Saturn is said to be "the Lord of Karma, the imposer of retribution and the one who demands full payment of all debts and who therefore condemns us to the struggle for existence, both from the form side and from the soul side."[55] And from the same source: "Saturn is one of the most potent of the four Lords of Karma and forces man to face up to the past and in the present to prepare for the future. Such is the intention and purpose of karmic opportunity."[56]

Unquestionably it was the Law of Karma to which the Christ referred in the following:

> MATTHEW 5:18: For verily I say unto you, Till heaven and earth pass, one jot or one tittle shall in no wise pass from the law, till all be fulfilled.
> MATTHEW 7:2: For with what judgment ye judge, ye shall be judged: and with what measure ye mete, it shall be measured to you again.

Also, it could be asserted that the Law of Karma is somewhat similar to Newton's third law of motion, to the effect that action and reaction are equal and opposite.

Those who teach the Law of Karma say that each person is responsible for his thoughts, feelings, speech, and actions and that eventually he will have to experience—on this dense physical plane—the effects of all the causes he has initiated thereon, until he learns to bring his entire being into line with spiritual Law.

Someone has pointed out that no man actually breaks God's law, for it is immutable; man but breaks himself against the Law. "Thus, like the revolutions of a wheel, there is a regular succession of death and birth, the moral cause of which is the cleaving to existing objects, while the instrumental cause is *karma* (the power which controls the universe, prompting it to activity), merit and demerit."[57]

---

[55] *Ibid.*, p. 105.
[56] *Ibid.*, p. 164.
[57] Blavatsky, *Isis Unveiled*, I, 346.

In order that some of the concepts in the following chapter may be more comprehensible, it has been deemed advisable to make very brief reference to the seven rays.

Esotericism teaches that there are in the cosmos seven great rays, of which one is in operation in this solar system. The endless variations of the seven subdivisions of this one ray are said to form everything which exists in this system. These seven subdivisions of the solar ray are called "the seven rays," comprehensive details concerning which are set forth in a five-volume series entitled *A Treatise on the Seven Rays,* by Alice A. Bailey (Lucis Publishing Company). In Volume I, page 316, a ray has been defined as follows: "*A ray is but a name for a particular force or type of energy, with the emphasis upon the quality which that force exhibits and not upon the form aspect which it creates. This is a true definition of a ray.*" [Italics as in original.]

Also there is the statement that ". . . it is not to humanity only that these rays apply, but to the seven kingdoms as well. In fact there is nothing in the whole solar system, at whatever stage of evolution it may stand, which does not belong and has not always belonged to one or other of the seven rays."[58]

Characteristics of these seven rays are set forth, as follows:

Ray I	Will or Power
Ray II	Love-Wisdom (balance, intuition)
Ray III	Active Intelligence (higher mind)
Ray IV	Harmony through Conflict
Ray V	Concrete Knowledge (lower mind)
Ray VI	Devotion and Idealism
Ray VII	Ceremonial Ritual (or order)

It is said further that the rays which must be considered as having the greatest conditioning power in the case of every individual man are those of (1) the solar system, (2) the Logos of the planet Earth, (3) the human kingdom itself, (4) the race (5) any particular cycle, (6) the nation, (7) the

---

[58] Alice A. Bailey, *Seven Rays,* I (Esoteric Psychology), 163.

soul, or ego, (8) the personality, and (9) those governing (*a*) the mental body, (*b*) the emotional or astral body, and (*c*) the physical body[59]

Therefore it may be seen, even by referring to such a thumb-nail sketch as that given directly above, that every person is far more complex in his energy-structure and is subject to many more influences than those ascribed by the physical scientists in their current definitions of heredity and environment. For example, it is conceivable that a human being's three outer vehicles of manifestation might be on three different rays, his personality on a fourth, his soul on a fifth, and his monad on a sixth. Since each ray is but a name for a particular force or type of energy emphasizing a quality, and since each ego in each life uses several bodies in addition to the dense physical, the energy combinations are endless.

It might be added that the energies that constitute the ray forces "do not come from the twelve constellations of the zodiac, but emanate primarily from a world of being and of consciousness which lies behind our solar system, and which themselves come from the seven constellations which form the body of manifestation of the One About Whom Naught May Be Said. Our solar system is one of these seven constellations. This is the world of Deity Itself, and of it a man can know nothing until he has passed through the major initiations."[60]

Two other terms that will be considered herein very briefly are *Initiation* and *Hierarchy*.

It has been stated that:

The word *Initiation* comes from two Latin words, *in*, into, and *ire*, to go; therefore, *the making of a beginning*, or the entrance into something. It posits, in its widest sense, in the case we are studying, an entrance into the spiritual life, or into a fresh stage in that life. It is the first step, and the succeeding steps, upon

---

[59] Condensed from Bailey, *Treatise on Seven Rays*, I, 333.
[60] Bailey, *Treatise on Seven Rays*, I, 332.

the Path of Holiness. Literally, therefore, a man who has taken
the first initiation is one who has taken the first step into the
spiritual kingdom, having passed out of the definitely human
kingdom into the superhuman.[61]

A further elucidation in the same volume, which is devoted
to the subject, states:

> Initiation, or the process of undergoing an expansion of con-
> sciousness, is part of the normal process of evolutionary develop-
> ment, viewed on a large scale, and not from the standpoint of the
> individual. When viewed from the individual standpoint it has
> come to be narrowed down to the moment wherein the evolving
> unit definitely apprehends that (by dint of his own effort, aided
> by the advice and suggestions of the watching Teachers of the
> race) he has reached a point wherein a certain range of knowledge
> of a subjective nature, from the physical plane point of view, is
> his.[62]

It is explained that at the first initiation, that of the birth
of the Christ within the individual, *"the heart centre* is the one
usually vivified, with the aim in view of the more effective
controlling of the astral [emotional] vehicle, and the rendering
of greater service to humanity."[63]

The second initiation is said to form the *crisis* in the control
of the astral or emotional body. While at the third initiation,
sometimes termed the transfiguration, the teaching shifts up-
ward to the next-higher plane and the individual learns to control his mental vehicle. It is during this initiation that the
entire personality is said to be flooded with light from above.
At the fourth initiation, or crucifixion, everything—including the
perfected personality—is laid upon the altar of sacrifice and the
initiate renounces "friends, money, reputation, character, standing in the world, family, and even life itself."[64]

---

[61] Bailey, *Initiation, Human and Solar,* p. 10 [Italics as in original.]
[62] *Ibid.,* pp. 12, 13.
[63] *Ibid.,* p. 84.
[64] *Ibid.,* p. 89.

"After the fifth initiation the man is perfected as far as this scheme goes, though he may, if he will, take two further initiations."[65]

Should anyone desire to pursue the subject more fully, it is suggested that he refer to the book *Initiation, Human and Solar*, by Alice A. Bailey, from which these extracts concerning initiation were taken, permission to quote having been granted by the New York headquarters of Lucis Publishing Company.

From the same source, which also refers to the Spiritual Hierarchy of this planet, the following is taken: "Our Hierarchy is a miniature replica of the greater synthesis of those selfconscious Entities who manipulate, control, and demonstrate through the sun and the seven sacred planets, as well as the other planets, greater and smaller, of which our solar system is composed."[66]

It is pointed out that the Hierarchy of the planet Earth has four pre-eminent lines of work: (1) to develop self-consciousness in all beings; (2) to develop consciousness in the three lower kingdoms; (3) to transmit the will of the planetary Logos, and (4) to set an example to humanity.

With regard to points 1 and 2 it is stated, in part: ". . . the five kingdoms of nature on the evolutionary arc might be defined as follows:—the mineral kingdom, the vegetable kingdom, the animal kingdom, the human kingdom, and the spiritual kingdom. *All these kingdoms embody some type of consciousness. . . .*"[67] [Italics are mine. H.B.D.]

Within the planetary Hierarchy, there are said to be three departmental heads: (1) the Manu, who reflects the will aspect; (2) the Bodhisattva (the Christ or World Teacher), who reflects the love-wisdom aspect, and (3) the Mahachohan (or Lord of Civilization), who reflects the intelligence aspect of the Lord of the World or the Ancient of Days. Under their direction work the Masters of the Wisdom.

---

[65] *Ibid.*, p. 90
[66] *Ibid.*, p. 20.
[67] *Ibid.*, p. 21.

The problem of good or evil, light or darkness, right or wrong, was enunciated solely for the benefit of humanity and to enable men to cast off the fetters which imprisoned spirit, and thus achieve spiritual freedom. This problem exists not in the kingdoms below man, nor for those who transcend the human. Man has to learn through experience and pain the fact of the duality of all existence. Having thus learnt, he chooses that which concerns the fully conscious spirit aspect of divinity, and learns to centre himself in that aspect. Having thus achieved liberation he finds indeed that all is one, that spirit and matter are a unity. . . .[68]

Again, the concept of polarity, but resolved into One.

The stated purpose of this book is not to convince anyone of anything or to convert anybody to any "new" idea; it is to search for truth and to provoke thought. With the above brief definitions in mind, the next chapter will attempt to discover a more logical—or at least a different—explanation for the act of Judas Iscariot than has been presented in the past, and its thoughts will be followed more easily now that the terminology has been clarified.

All men are said to be created equal spiritually. But physically, emotionally, mentally, and personality-wise there undoubtedly are as many variations as there are human beings.

If it is granted that all expressions of God Immanent are evolving and that no two are identical, then it follows automatically that all units—including those in the human kingdom —are at differing points of consciousness, levels of development, degrees of complexity and/or refinement. Such a conclusion should be self-evident from observation alone.

Which could bring up the question: where might Judas Iscariot have been, *in consciousness,* with relation to the other eleven Apostles? Only a Master of the Wisdom might be qualified to answer, but even so, He would not—unless the Law allowed. Nevertheless it *is* permissible for human beings to

---

[68] *Ibid.,* pp. 34, 35.

speculate about things they do not understand; otherwise there would be no need for mind and man would be an automaton.

It is perhaps safe to say that for twenty centuries Judas has been considered as the lowest, or the last, or as having the least development, of the Twelve. Arguing from premises that were held to be sound, no other conclusion could have been reached.

However, every thinking person knows that logic and truth do not always coincide.

CHAPTER 12

The Twelfth Apostle

He then having received the sop went immediately out: and it was night.
Therefore, when he was gone out, Jesus said, Now is the Son of man glorified, and God is glorified in him.   —JOHN 13:30,31

THE READER, for his own edification, might like to attempt to answer the following questions prior to plunging into the concepts which will be posited subsequently. How could Judas Iscariot . . .

. . . if he were an ordinary man, have been chosen to bear such a heavy load of negative karma, in order that one of the Scriptures might be fulfilled?

. . . have been given knowledge about the mystery of the kingdom of God, and yet be a rank materialist?

. . . have preached, healed, and exorcised evil spirits by virtue of the authority of the Christ, and still believe that Jesus was interested in establishing a political kingdom on earth?

. . . have been called a thief, without explanation or supporting evidence of any kind?

. . . have betrayed Someone who "knew the hearts of all men" and who had predicted on at least five occasions that He was going to be betrayed?

. . . have been concerned, if indeed he were a traitor, to the point of cautioning the soldiers to lead his Teacher away "safely"?

. . . have betrayed the Lord only after the Last Supper, when all the arrangements had been made several days earlier?

. . . have been addressed as "Friend" by the One he is said to have betrayed?

. . . have delivered Jesus to the chief priests and still, apparently, never have testified against Him?

. . . have repented and, seemingly, never have been forgiven to this very day by loving Christians?

. . . have returned the thirty pieces of silver to the priests and at the same time have used them to purchase a field?

. . . have hanged himself and still have managed to have fallen headlong, have burst asunder in the midst, and have all of his bowels gush out?

These twelve questions are serious inquiries that might come to the mind of anyone who compared the four Gospels (as well as Acts 1:15–26) in order to try to understand Judas Iscariot. The deeper the search, the more puzzling and seemingly contradictory the answers. Possible solutions to some of the queries have been attempted in earlier chapters, and an effort has been made to resolve a few of the apparent contradictions.

But what about the first question on the list: How could Judas Iscariot, if he were an ordinary man, have been chosen to bear such a heavy load of negative karma in order that one of the Scriptures might be fulfilled? Would the Christ—who is the embodiment of the principle and energy of love—have selected just any person within the strictly human kingdom who was capable of betrayal to ensure that such work would be done? At that time and in that area there must have been hundreds—perhaps thousands—of men who were not evolved beyond the point of betrayal. Would the Lord have saddled any such individual with that sort of karmic debt?

And consider the second question: How could Judas have been given knowledge of the kingdom of God and yet be a rank materialist? Jesus is reported to have told his disciples (Matthew 13:11,13–16):

. . . it is given unto you to know the mysteries of the kingdom of heaven, but to them it is not given. . . .

Therefore speak I unto them in parables: because they seeing see not; and hearing they hear not, neither do they understand.

And in them is fulfilled the prophecy of Esaias, which saith, By hearing ye shall hear, and shall not understand; and seeing ye shall see, and shall not perceive.

For this people's heart is waxed gross, and their ears are dull of hearing, and their eyes they have closed; lest at any time they should see with their eyes, and hear with their ears, and should understand with their heart, and should be converted, and I should heal them.

But blessed are your eyes, for they see: and your ears, for they hear. [Italics are mine. H.B.D.]

From this quotation it is clear that Jesus considered the disciples to be different from the masses of men. Note the last sentence. He said in effect that they were able to see and hear the meaning behind the mysteries which He told them privately and not in parables. Not only was Judas one of His disciples; he was one of the inner council of twelve. As such, he was one of those who received the highest teaching from the Master. Would the Lord have given such instruction—would He have imparted such sacred information—to a man whose heart He *knew* had "waxed gross," whose ears were "dull of hearing," whose eyes were "closed"? It is said that only to Initiates is such revelation made. If this is so, it follows that Judas Iscariot was an Initiate of the Mysteries and not an ordinary man.

Now, if Judas were an Initiate, he would have been fully aware that the Master had no intention of becoming a political ruler. And if Judas were an Initiate, he himself would have had no interest in becoming secretary of the treasury or in holding any similar post, for his whole trend of thought would have been in the opposite direction.

Further, were Judas initiated into the mysteries of the kingdom of God he most definitely would not have been capable of theft, for one does not reach that grade or degree of initiation until such crude traits have been completely eliminated from the personality.

How could Judas Iscariot have betrayed Someone who knew the hearts of all men and who had predicted on at least five occasions that He was going to be betrayed? *By its very nature, betrayal presupposes trust on the part of the one betrayed.* How would it be possible for anyone to deceive a person "who knew all men"?

Very frequently in the Gospels the word "deliver" is used as a synonym for the word "betray." Isn't it conceivable that writers, scribes, copiers, translators, or later dogmatists may have used the term "betray" for the reason that Judas's act appeared as betrayal to them? Might it not have been so intended, since betrayal (being a pitfall upon the path to holiness) needed to be dramatized in order that it might be avoided or overcome by men?

Touched upon earlier were the queries regarding Judas's command to lead his Teacher away "safely" and Judas's financial arrangement with the chief priests prior to the Last Supper. But why did Jesus address Judas as "Friend"? This has been explained as being an example of the Lord's great compassion, of His infinite capacity for forgiveness. Apparently it has occurred to no one that Jesus might have been addressing Judas as a friend for the simple reason that he *was* His friend.

Even more astonishing is the following oversight: How could Judas Iscariot have delivered Jesus to the chief priests and still, evidently, never have testified against Him? Particularly when it is written in Mark (14:55,56): *"And the chief priests and all the council sought for witness against Jesus to put him to death; and found none. For many bare false witness against him, but their witness agreed not together."* (Italics added.) Where was the so-called traitor? Who could have provided better, more reliable, or a greater amount of testimony than Judas in the eyes of the chief priests? Had he wished to serve as a witness against his Master, anything he might have invented would have been believed by most of the members of the Sanhedrin. Note that the chief priests and all the council sought for some witness to provide the testimony upon which Jesus could be condemned to death "and found none." Where was Judas?

The eleventh question poses an apparent unsolvable contradiction, for in Matthew (27:3-10) Judas returned the money to the priests, who bought with it the field in which to bury strangers, while in Acts (1:18) it appears as if Judas himself purchased the field with the "reward of his iniquity."

It is puzzling to try to answer the twelfth question, for in Matthew (27:5) Judas "went and hanged himself", whereas in Acts (1:18), "falling headlong, he burst asunder in the midst, and all his bowels gushed out." As previously stated, some authorities have attempted to reconcile these statements by suggesting that the limb or branch of the tree on which Judas hanged himself broke and crashed to the ground, thereby causing him to "burst asunder." Would that such authorities could as readily discover how Judas bought the field with money that he is said to have returned to the priests.

Dr. H. Spencer Lewis, in *The Secret Doctrines of Jesus,* marshals considerable evidence to support the theory that Jesus and His group constituted a secret society or mystery school. One of the factors cited is that there were at least two levels of teaching, as stated by Jesus himself (Matthew 13:10-16 and Mark 4:10-12): one for the disciples and another—parables—for the people. There may have been a third level for the Twelve Apostles, who, by virtue of their spiritual evolvement, were able to absorb deeper truths and who had in past lives earned the right to such a privilege.

If Dr. Lewis is right and the earliest Christians were studying the ancient wisdom as members of an esoteric school, they were bound by voluntary oath to secrecy. Assuming tentatively this premise, it is interesting to note that there is no biblical record that Judas—although he is said to have pointed out Jesus to His enemies—either revealed any of the inner teaching or testified against the Teacher. And this, despite the fact that *all* the council was *searching* for a witness.

One wonders if there is any need to point out that in a mystery school (or in any school, for that matter) the students are not necessarily on the same level of consciousness. Within any given grade or class, there are varying degrees of understanding and awareness.

Also, it has been observed that the higher the Initiate, the less the tendency on the part of most people to recognize His status. Take the Christ as an example: in those years, undoubtedly there was no higher Initiate working openly among the masses and yet—despite His teaching, the demonstration of His life, and His miracles—out of a crowd of about 5,000, approximately 120 may have "recognized" Him, at least to some degree. This figures to .024, or 2.4 per cent. One wonders what the ratio would be today.

To disgress for a moment, have you ever thought whether or not you would recognize the Christ if He reappeared in current garb? When He walked among men almost two thousand years ago, He dressed according to the period and region. He was not conspicuously attired or mention would have been made of it in the Gospels. In other words, He did not wear an animal skin as did the cave men. He was not dressed as a Chinese sage or an Indian prince. Nor did He appear as a knight in shining armor or an astronaut from a future century. Is there any reason to assume that He will use a radically different technique during His second coming? In all probability He will look like a modern man. Gone may be the sweeping robes, the sandals, the flowing hair, perhaps the beard. And—when one stops to think about it—is there any reason why He must appear in the field of religion? Suppose He were active in government, finance, science, one of the arts, or education. How many would recognize Him? Would most people not react as did the Pharisees and the Sadducees, but on a higher curve of the spiral?

There are those who will object to the suggestion that the Christ might appear in some field other than that of religion. "He is a spiritual leader," they will say, "therefore it is reasonable to expect that He will labor in the spiritual vineyard and will work through the church." And they will mean the Christian church, no doubt. But . . . which one? And is not the entire world the spiritual vineyard?

A very great Teacher has said: "That is spiritual which lies beyond the point of present achievement; it is that which embodies the vision and which urges the man on towards a goal higher than the one attained."[69] The Teacher states that the word "spiritual" covers every phase of living experience. In the light of this definition, is there any field today that could be considered more spiritual than that of right education?

But to return to Judas: he could not possibly have shirked in fulfilling his share of the teaching, preaching, healing, etc., which the Twelve were sent out—in pairs—by Jesus to do. One has every right to assume that, had he reneged in any way, such failure would have been recorded, especially in view of his subsequent action, which has been referred to as the betrayal.

Again: if (as Dr. Lewis suggests) Jesus headed an esoteric school, if there were about 120 members divided into groups of ten, and if each apostle headed such a group, then Judas Iscariot had under his supervision and guidance nine lesser disciples. This would mean that each of the Twelve Apostles had a share in teaching those on the Path, in addition to preaching to men in the outer world. Now, as any teacher of any subject at any level will substantiate, a person learns by teaching. For in order to teach something to someone else, it is necessary first to clarify the concept in one's own mind and secondly to find the words and analogies that will make communication possible. Then in the interplay of ideas between teacher and pupil additional light is cast on the subject which is of value to both. This further possibility for gaining understanding—in addition to listening, observing, and experimenting

---

[69] Alice A. Bailey, *Discipleship in the New Age* (New York: Lucis Publishing Company), II, 234.

—makes it all the more difficult to credit the contention that Judas did not comprehend the spiritual nature of the Christ's mission.

Turning once more to the Gospel of John, chapter 13, verses 21 through 31 (Table VII), one reads that after the footwashing Jesus is reported to have said: "Verily, verily, I say unto you, that one of you shall betray me." After which the disciples looked at one another "doubting of whom he spake." Then Simon Peter is said to have beckoned to the disciple who was leaning on Jesus' bosom, the one "whom Jesus loved" (who generally is thought to have been John), to have him ask "who it should be of whom he spake." Whereupon that disciple inquired of Jesus, "Lord, who is it?" To which Jesus answered, "He it is to whom I shall give a sop, when I have dipped it. And when he had dipped the sop, he gave it to Judas Iscariot, the son of Simon." The balance of the quotation from John 13 follows:

> 27 And after the sop Satan entered into him. Then said Jesus unto him, That thou doest, do quickly.
> 28 Now no man at the table knew for what intent he spake this unto him.
> 29 For some of them thought, because Judas had the bag, that Jesus had said unto him, Buy those things that we have need of against the feast; or, that he should give something to the poor.
> 30 He then having received the sop went immediately out: and it was night.
> 31 Therefore, when he was gone out, Jesus said, Now is the Son of man glorified, and God is glorified in him.

One cannot help but wonder why any of the eleven Apostles should think that Jesus had told Judas to buy those things they had "need of against the feast" when the supper was already ended. John's Gospel so states at the beginning of the same chapter. In verse 2 thereof it is said: "And supper being ended . . ." while the opening words of verse 4 are "He riseth from supper . . ."

However, assuming that some additional item may have

been required, the following question comes to mind: "Why should any of the inner Twelve have been asked to run an errand for food at such a critical time?" Certainly, Judas "had the bag." But if he were told that something was needed, is it not more reasonable that he would have called in a junior disciple and given him instructions about what to purchase and the money wherewith to procure it?

And why—on such a momentous occasion—would Judas have been asked to leave in order to "give something to the poor"? Particularly in view of the following statements in Luke (22:14, 15): "And when the hour was come, he sat down, and the twelve apostles with him. And he said unto them, With desire I have desired to eat this passover with you before I suffer."

Is it not most difficult to credit either of the above-quoted explanations?

And *if*—as has been proposed—the Twelve were members of the inner council of an arcane school headed by the Christ, it is the author's personal opinion that verse 29 of chapter 13 of John is totally unbelievable.

Probably because of the prior statement, "Now no man at the table knew for what intent he spake this unto him," people have tried to explain the perplexity of the Apostles by saying that Jesus whispered or murmured His reply to the query, "Lord, who is it?" But the Bible does not state, or even imply, that Jesus' answer was given in a whisper. The phrase about the apostle "leaning on Jesus' bosom" undoubtedly contributed to that conclusion. The Lord may, indeed, have whispered or have spoken in a soft voice, but since He had been addressing all present, this is unlikely. The other Gospels indicate questioning on the part of the Twelve, each asking "Is it I?"

In Luke (22:23,24) there is a curious linkage of thought at this point: "And they began to inquire among themselves, which of them it was that should do this thing. And there was also a strife among them, which of them should be accounted the greatest." One cannot help but wonder why the discussion about which apostle was going to betray the Master should trigger a debate concerning which of them should be greatest.

Reverting to John's Gospel: "And after the sop Satan entered into him. Then Jesus said unto him, That thou doest, do quickly." There is no indication whatever that Judas attempted in any way to defend himself against the implication that he was to be the betrayer. Would you say that this was a normal behavior-response?

"He then having received the sop, went immediately out: and it was night." There is something about this verse that is disturbing. If you had been planning to betray someone and that person named you in front of your intimate friends, what would be your immediate—almost reflex—reaction? Would you not deny the inference? Would you not dispute about it? Would you not affirm your undying loyalty? Would you not try to convince your accuser, and more particularly your friends, that you most assuredly were not that type of person? But Judas did none of these things. He went immediately out.

It is almost as if there were an agreement between Jesus and Judas.

Of course, it could be argued that Judas knew he was the betrayer because he had made the arrangements with the chief priests several days previously. But making arrangements and knowing what one is planning to do are entirely different things from facing the person one is about to betray, especially when that person has just announced one's plan in front of one's very good friends. Judas Iscariot's reaction patterns were not what might be expected under the circumstances. Why? Did he leave quickly so as not to have to face his friends? Perhaps he left in haste in order not to have to answer questions or because he was ashamed. These are possible answers. But is it reasonable that he would say nothing at all to his Teacher—offer no denial, give no excuse, make no pretense?

Could it be possible that Judas Iscariot had *volunteered* to deliver Jesus into the hands of the chief priests, in order that the prophecy might be fulfilled?

In this connection, it should be remembered that Jesus

had predicted on not one but several occasions that He would be "betrayed" or "delivered" into the hands of men who would kill him. He also made it clear that He would rise again on the third day.

Luke (18:31) states: "Then he took unto him *the twelve,* and said unto them, Behold, we go up to Jerusalem, and all things that are written by the prophets concerning the Son of man shall be accomplished."

In Matthew (26:56), when the multitude went to the Garden of Gethsemane with swords and staves to take Him, the following words are credited to Jesus: "But all this was done that the scriptures of the prophets might be fulfilled."

And in John (13:31), in the very next verse after that which states that Judas had left, it is written: "Therefore, when he was gone out, Jesus said, *Now* is the Son of man glorified, and God is glorified in him."

Identifying Jesus for His enemies seems to have been an essential part of the plan of the Spiritual Hierarchy. In order to fulfill the Scriptures, and possibly because men needed to have the negative polarity vividly portrayed, someone had to "deliver" or "betray" (biblically, the words are used interchangeably) Jesus to His enemies.

What is the real significance of the following words of the Lord, as quoted in John (13:18): *"I know whom I have chosen: but that the scripture may be fulfilled,* he that eateth bread with me hath lifted up his heel against me"? [Italics are mine. H.B.D.]

Then there is the matter of the kingdoms. In Luke (22:28–30) one reads:

> Ye are they which have continued with me in my temptations.
> And I appoint unto you a kingdom, as my Father hath appointed unto me;
> That ye may eat and drink at my table in my kingdom, and sit on thrones judging the twelve tribes of Israel.

This was said during the Last Supper and no mention is made

in Luke that Judas Iscariot had left the Upper Room. Besides, as mentioned earlier, would Jesus be telling *eleven* Apostles that they would be judging *twelve* tribes?

When one reads the Scriptures in the light of the thought that Judas Iscariot *may have offered* or *may have been selected* to serve the Master in the way that he did, one finds many verses that could be interpreted in an entirely different fashion from the way in which they have been over the last twenty centuries.

For instance, there is the recurrent theme of the Apostles' disputing among themselves as to which of them should be greatest. Now, most people would say that this was a perfectly normal aspiration and doubtless the Apostles are loved all the more because they exhibited such a human trait. But it is somewhat startling to discover that these discussions invariably followed the Lord's prophecies concerning His eventual betrayal and death.

And tied in with them closely were Jesus' teachings that "whosoever will save his life shall lose it: and whosoever will lose his life for my sake shall find it" (Matthew 16:25; Mark 8:35; Luke 9:24); "And he sat down *and called the twelve*, and saith unto them, If any man desire to be first; the same shall be last of all, and servant of all" (Mark 9:35); "And he said unto them . . . for he that is least among you all, the same shall be great" (Luke 9:48); ". . . but whosoever will be great among you, let him be your minister; and whosoever will be chief among you, let him be your servant: even as the Son of man came not to be ministered unto, but to minister, and to give his life a ransom for many" (Matthew 20:26-28, Mark 10:43-45); ". . . he that is greatest among you, let him be as the younger, and he that is chief, as he that doth serve" (Luke 22:26).

Is it merely coincidental that these three ideas—the prediction of Jesus' betrayal and death, the dispute as to which apostle should be greatest, and the teaching that the first shall be last—are recorded repeatedly in such proximity? May there not have been a reason for their having been thus related? Would the Christ do anything haphazardly, capriciously, "accidentally," or without purpose? If not, what might His purpose have been? Among other reasons, could He have been testing the Apostles' spiritual understanding and discernment? May He have been planting seeds within their minds and hearts, knowing that ultimately at least one seed would fall upon "good ground"—that some Apostle would see the relation between what had to be done and one method of discipleship service? Could Judas have been that Apostle? Or is it perhaps more conceivable that several—or even all—of them eventually came to understand that the one who would help to fulfill the Scriptures by "delivering" the Teacher into the hands of men would be contributing to the working out of the plan through the "lowest" possible type of action? In other words, such a man would be "the last of all and servant of all." And since Jesus had said, ". . . whosoever will be chief among you, let him be your servant," perhaps they were contending or competing to do this service.

When the Christ stated during the Last Supper, "Verily I say unto you, that one of you, shall betray me," and they "began every one of them to say unto him, Lord, is it I?" they may have been awaiting His announcement as to which of them He had chosen to perform the "necessary but regrettable act."

However, provided all Twelve had offered to execute this difficult commission and thankless (from the standpoint of humanity), there frequently is a great gap between *wanting* to do something and *being able* to do it. Often "the spirit indeed is willing, but the flesh is weak," as the Lord has said. The statement in John (13:18), "I know whom I have chosen: but that the scripture may be fulfilled," might refer to the possibility that out of a maximum of twelve applicants, Jesus—after weighing their qualifications—had selected the Apostle who, in His estimation, was most likely to be able to carry through.

As evidence that individuals do desire and offer to do things for which they are not prepared, there is Simon Peter, who, according to Luke (22:33,34), said: "Lord, I am ready to go with thee, both into prison, and to death." To which zealous and perfectly sincere offer Jesus replied, "I tell thee, Peter, the cock shall not crow this day, before that thou shalt thrice deny that thou knowest me." And it was so.

The suggestion that there may have been twelve volunteers for the enactment of "betrayal" appears to be contradicted by the statement in John (13:28): "Now no man at the table knew for what intent he spake this unto him" (unto Judas). But there are other New Testament passages that seem to confirm the idea, when read in this new light.

In talking with Peter, after He had washed the feet of the Apostles on the night of the Last Supper, Jesus is reported by John (13:10,11) to have said: "He that is washed needeth not save to wash his feet, but is clean every whit: and *ye are clean, but not all.* For he knew who should betray him; therefore said he, Ye are not all clean." [Italics are mine. H.B.D.]

Again, the latter idea has the ring of having been "skipped in," for when the Lord said, ". . . ye are clean, but not all," He may very well have meant that the Apostles—all of the Apostles—needed further purification, prior to taking higher initiations. He could have had in mind that they were not all clean or completely clean, rather than (as the second sentence implies) that Judas was the only unclean member of the group.

The sop which Jesus gave to Judas after the Last Supper may have been nothing more than an outward symbol of His decision. Or it could have been a signal to Judas to begin the last phase of his work. The verse (John 13:27) reads: "And after the sop Satan entered into him. Then said Jesus unto him, That thou doest, do quickly." Note that first Judas received the sop from Jesus. Next, Satan entered into Judas. And third, Jesus told him to make haste. What possible connection, if any, was there between the reception of the sop and the entering of Satan?

To date, almost everyone has assumed that Satan tempted Judas to betray the Lord. Such a conclusion is strengthened by Luke (22:3,4): "Then entered Satan into Judas surnamed Iscariot, being of the number of the twelve. And he went his way, and communed with the chief priests and captains, how he might betray him unto them." But in neither of the above references does the Bible state that Satan entered into Judas *in order to tempt him to betray the Christ*. The wording is "Satan entered into him" and "then entered Satan into Judas." And because it follows that Jesus said, "That thou doest, do quickly," or that Judas "went his way, and communed with the chief priests how he might betray him unto them," it has been inferred that Satan's function was to tempt Judas to betray the Master. But that is not what these quotations say. They state only that Satan entered into Judas.

That Satan was tempting Judas there is no question. But *in what manner?* Could it be that he was tempting Judas *not* to go through with the act of betrayal?

When a person stops really to think about the matter, the idea occurs: why should Satan tempt Judas to go through with something that would benefit the plan of the Spiritual Hierarchy and fulfill the ancient scriptural prophecies? He would be doing himself no good thereby. He would be working against his own interests. As Jesus is reported to have said in Luke (11:18): "If Satan also be divided against himself, how shall his kingdom stand?"

There is one verse, however, which appears to provide a scriptural basis for the belief that Satan's purpose was to tempt Judas to betray Jesus (in the manner in which the story has been interpreted for the last two thousand years). The verse may be found in John (13:2): "And supper being ended, the devil having now put into the heart of Judas Iscariot, Simon's son, to betray him . . ."

To betray Him, yes. But again, *in what manner?*

By tempting Judas to betray Jesus (in the conventional sense of the word), Satan would have been helping to bring divine prophecy to fulfillment, in order that the Son of man be glorified and that God be glorified in Him (John 13:31). Is it the work of the so-called devil *directly* to aid the Christ and the Brotherhood of Light? Is Satan not supposed to be the Adversary?

If anyone has doubts that the entire drama, including the "betrayal," was preplanned or preordained, let that person recall the words of Jesus as set forth in Matthew (26:53,54): "Thinkest thou that I cannot now pray to my Father, and he shall presently give me more than twelve legions of angels? *But how then shall the scriptures be fulfilled, that thus, it must be?*" as well as Matthew (26:56): "*But all this was done that the scriptures of the prophets might be fulfilled.*" And in John (13:18): "*I know whom I have chosen: but that the scripture may be fulfilled*"; also the Lord's statement immediately after Judas had left the Upper Room (John 13:31): "Therefore, *when he was gone out,* Jesus said, *Now* is the Son of man glorified, and God is glorified in him." [Italics are mine. H.B.D.]

When people go to a Christian church to receive communion, a sacred wafer is given them in order, among other reasons, that they might be strengthened to resist "the world, the flesh, and the devil." Could the sop have been given to Judas for the same reason? Did it help him to resist the temptation *not* to carry out the "necessary but regrettable act"? Did the words of Jesus, "That thou doest, do quickly," provide Judas with added strength and encouragement?

Was the sop given and were these words spoken in order that Judas might *not* falter?

Rereading, in the light of the above possibilities, the story about Jesus' arrest in the Garden of Gethsemane, entirely different interpretations may result with regard to the "kiss" and to the word "Friend."

For example, in Matthew (26:49,50) it is said: "And forthwith he came to Jesus, and said, Hail, master; and kissed him. And Jesus said unto him, Friend, wherefore art thou come?"

Hasn't the enquiry "wherefore art thou come?" been difficult to comprehend, especially when it is written that Jesus knew everything that was going to happen to Him and personally had sent Judas on his way to accomplish this very arrest? Why, then, should He be asking Judas such an enigmatical question?

Considering the hypotheses set forth in this chapter, one can now begin to understand how Judas could have said, "Hail, master," and have kissed the One he was "betraying." Judas may have thought that this might very well have been the last time he would have an opportunity to speak to, or be close to, his Teacher on the dense physical plane in that particular incarnation. While the words "wherefore art thou come?" attributed to Jesus could mean: "Why did you torture yourself by coming all the way with these people? You could have simply pointed me out to them."

In Mark (14:44,45) it is related: "And he that had betrayed him gave them a token, saying, Whomsoever I shall kiss, that same is he; take him, and lead him away safely. And as soon as he was come, he goeth straightway to him, and saith, Master, master; and kissed him." Why did Judas use that particular "token" to identify Jesus? Might it not be because he loved Him? The words "Master, master" may have been wrung from the very soul of the man.

When one turns to Luke (22:47,48)—"And while he yet spake, behold a multitude, and he that was called Judas, one of the twelve, went before them, and drew near unto Jesus to kiss him. But Jesus said unto him, Judas, betrayest thou the Son of man with a kiss?"—the idea that Judas could have had deep love for his Teacher seems even more valid. For *if Judas Iscariot had volunteered and had been selected* to "deliver" the Master into the hands of the multitude, then might not Jesus have been warning him that kissing the person one is betraying is out of character?

However, in John (18:3–9), the story changes: therein Judas not only does not kiss Jesus, nor attempt to kiss Him, but stands with the crowd *while Jesus identifies Himself, not once but twice*:

Judas then, having received a band of men and officers from the chief priests and Pharisees, cometh thither with lanterns and torches and weapons.

Jesus therefore, knowing all things that should come upon him, went forth, and said unto them, Whom seek ye?

They answered him, Jesus of Nazareth. Jesus saith unto them, I am he. *And Judas* also, which betrayed him, *stood with them.*

As soon as he had said unto them, I am he, they went backward, and fell to the ground.

Then asked he them again, Whom seek ye? And they said, Jesus of Nazareth.

Jesus answered, I have told you that I am he: if therefore ye seek me, let these go their way;

That the saying might be fulfilled which he spake, Of them which thou gavest me have I lost none.

About the word "Friend," which Jesus used according to Matthew in addressing Judas in the garden that fateful night, one can only ask why Judas should not have been called a friend if he were performing this necessary act voluntarily. And IF it were required that Judas—in order to portray betrayal so as to dramatize for humanity the self-destructive aspect of betrayal—had to take his own life, then the statement of the Christ in the Gospel of St. John (15:13) should be called to mind: "Greater love hath no man than this, that a man lay down his life for his friends."

Assuming that Judas did volunteer and had been chosen to perform this "necessary but regrettable act," how could he have gone through with it? What manner of man was Judas? If, indeed, he loved the Lord, how could he have brought himself to the point of being the instrument through which the Christ was captured and later tormented and crucified? What kind of love was this?

There is a love which considers the greatest good for the largest number. But those who are so fortunate as to love like this often have to sacrifice personal attachments in the interest of the greater whole.

Could John have completed such a mission, were it assigned

to him? Would devotion to Jesus have gotten in John's way? Did he possess enough of the requisite ray-quality?

Would Simon Peter have been able to carry such a commission to completion? What might have gotten in Peter's way? Was his astral nature as yet sufficiently stabilized?

What about Thomas? Would doubt have gotten in his way? Was he advanced to the point of conviction?

Since little actually is known about the personalities of the other Apostles, speculation about them in this matter would prove futile.

It would take a certain type of man to handle such a task. He would need to have been at a relatively high point in consciousness, but that in itself would not necessarily have been enough—for undoubtedly all in the inner group were highly evolved for that period. He would have had to have a nature which was mentally polarized to the point of being able to conceive of abstractions, to link cause and effect, to see purpose and plan, to think in large and general terms. He would have needed to have not only a sense of responsibility and a cool, keen intellect, but the ability to intuit higher truth. From an emotional standpoint, he would have had to be able to view the act impersonally or with detachment in order to control his own reactions. There is a possibility that he may have had a goodly portion of First Ray in his make-up, for that is said to be the energy of Spiritual Will or Power, having to do with the purpose of Deity or "divine incentive." In short, Judas Iscariot not only would have had to comprehend the *need* for the act, but he also would have had to have been possessed of the *will* or of those energy-combinations which would have enabled him to accomplish it.

Should the premises postulated in this chapter have any basis in fact, then Judas—instead of being the lowest—may have been one of the highest of the Christ's Apostles.

To revert briefly to an incident several days prior to the Last Supper, Luke states that Satan entered into Judas when he went to consult with the chief priests. If Satan were tempting him *not* to go through with the planned arrangements, Judas at that time had the inner strength to resist the temptation. He went his way and communed with the priests. But after the Last Supper Jesus may have given Judas the sop, knowing that he would need additional spiritual energy to conquer a similar but far more powerful test.

For the curtain was about to rise again upon the drama of the ages. In the next act, the Master was to be delivered into the hands of those who would humiliate and finally crucify Him. Treason and treachery were about to be manifested, since the negative polarity—as well as the positive—evidently had to be portrayed.

According to Matthew (27:1–10), after Judas's role in the great redemptive drama had been enacted, when he saw that Jesus had been condemned, the Twelfth Apostle "repented himself" and "cast down the thirty pieces of silver in the temple, and departed, and went and hanged himself."

Provided it were deemed necessary for Judas to take his life in order to set a shocking example to men of the self destructive nature of betrayal, then perhaps it was not exactly repentance that swept over Judas but a heavy sorrow concerning his Teacher and the full impact of the enormity of his act.

However, it is the opinion of this author that the Spiritual Hierarchy of the planet would have neither suggested nor condoned suicide. Hence, if the basic ideas in this book reflect even faintly a deeper level of the One Truth, this writer feels that some other interpretation concerning the closing biblical statements in the Judas story will one day enter the minds of men.

At this point it might be well to consider the following quotation from the scholarly work of Manly P. Hall, entitled *An Encyclopedic Outline of Masonic, Hermetic, Qabbalistic and Rosicrucian Symbolical Philosophy*: "The scorpion is the symbol of both wisdom and self-destruction. It was called by the Egyptians the creature accursed; the time of year when the sun entered the sign of Scorpio marked the beginning of the rulership of Typhon. When the twelve signs of the zodiac were used to represent the twelve Apostles (although the reverse is true), the scorpion was assigned to Judas Iscariot—the betrayer."[70]

It has been said that it is through the constellation Scorpio that the testing of the world disciple, humanity, is brought about. There can be little question that no one could proceed from the fourth, or human, kingdom into the fifth, or spiritual, kingdom who is capable of betrayal, not solely of associates on the outer plane but of the Christ principle within. The tendency to betray is identifiable with the outer man or developing personality which at its peak is selfish, individualistic, and separative in nature and which must become increasingly selfless and group-conscious during the process of evolutionary unfoldment.

Someone undoubtedly will recall that in Chapter 10 Judas's name was linked with the zodiacal sign Leo. There may be no real disagreement, however, because therein it was stated, "Judas, of the *tribe* of Judah (Leo)," whereas the quotation above assigns Scorpio to Judas, the *man.*

Still another source has said that Judas Iscariot symbolized, or stood for, the zodiacal sign at the time in power, the other eleven Apostles representing the remaining signs through which the sun must pass.

Isn't it a sad commentary that in a religion that teaches love and that definitely states "Judge not, that ye be not judged," the vast majority of people—if they do not actively hate Judas —most assuredly do judge him? But whether Judas Iscariot did what he did because he was an average or unperfected man or because he was considerably evolved or an Initiate of relatively high standing, the fact remains that since the Scriptures had to be fulfilled, there must have been a plan to be carried out.

---

[70] Manly P. Hall, *An Encyclopedic Outline of Masonic, Hermetic, Qabbalistic and Rosicrucian Symbolical Philosophy,* 11th ed. (Los Angeles: Philosophical Research Society, Inc.), p. LXXXVII.

If so, it appears that the delivering of the Christ into the hands of His enemies was an integral part of that plan.

Through the years there have been people who have tried sincerely to discover why Judas betrayed the Christ. They have attempted to find excuses for him, or higher motives for his action. Perhaps some of the kindest things that have been said about Judas are that he was so devoted to the Master that his blundering scheming resulted in the crucifixion and/or that he was an instrument of such a low degree of intelligence and such a high degree of selfishness that he could be used, like the thirty pieces of silver, in order that the Scriptures might be fulfilled.

Only to the evolved consciousness—to the Initiate—are the Mysteries said to be revealed. Men have every right to *believe* whatever they want to believe, but will any member of the strictly human kingdom claim that he *knows* why Judas acted in the way that he did? Doubtless there are people who, being unable as yet to discriminate between opinion and fact, will make such an assertion in all earnestness. However, a truly thoughtful person would pause and reflect upon the statement that Judas "will play his role in human evolution until such time as the lower nature of the race shall be redeemed."[71]

When humanity shall have become cognizant of the devastation wrought by betrayal—within both the individual and the fourth kingdom as a whole—and when redemptive measures shall have been established, then the act of Judas will have served its purpose fully.

No matter from what angle one looks at the story of the Twelfth Apostle, three points are indisputable:

It is written that the Lord said: *"I know whom I have chosen: but that the scripture may be fulfilled. . . ."*

There was a terrible, regrettable, heart-rending, but necessary job to be done.

And Judas Iscariot did it.

---

[71] *The New Age Bible Interpretation* (Oceanside, Calif.: New Age Press, Inc.), Vol. IV, Part II, p. 82.

Epilogue

". . . If the statements meet with eventual corroboration, or are deemed true under the test of the Law of Correspondences, then that is well and good. But should this not be so, let not the student accept what is said."

Closing sentences of the
Extract from a Statement by the Tibetan,
published in the books of Alice A. Bailey

Acknowledgments

To the Lord Buddha, the Lord Christ, the Master M., the Master D. K., the Master Jesus, and other members of the Spiritual Hierarchy of this planet; as well as to all individuals, teachers, and schools (both academic and arcane) on the dense physical plane; and to the Holy Bible, other world Scriptures, and countless good books—who and which have contributed so greatly to my present level of understanding—I offer my deepest gratitude.

Also, my sincere thanks are hereby extended to those listed below, who, in having generously granted permission to reprint various extracts, are in no way responsible for the context in which their quotations appear. In other words, because excerpts from other books are used in this volume for purposes of clarification and comparison, it does *not* follow that either their authors or their publishers condone or subscribe to the ideas and suggestions presented herein. For not one of these people knew the identity of the biblical figure about whom I was writing, much less the nature of what I was planning to say.

For such kind permissions and for the valuable material quoted, I am indebted to the following persons, publishers, and publications (listed in the order in which passages from their works appear in this volume):

Gertrude Hecht, manager of University Books, Inc., of New Hyde Park, N.Y., publishers of the 1961 edition of *Osiris, the Egyptian Religion of Resurrection*, written by E. A. Wallis Budge, late keeper of Egyptian antiquities in the British Museum, and also of *An Encyclopaedia of Occultism* by Lewis Spence.

K. N. Ramanathan, manager of The Theosophical Publishing

House, Adyar, Madras, India, holders of the copyright to the 1928 reprinting of the third edition of *The Secret Doctrine* by H. P. Blavatsky, and also to F. M. Maxwell of The Theosophical Publishing House London Ltd. of London, England, publishers of that particular edition.

Rona Klein of the reference department of Random House, Inc., New York, N.Y., publishers of the unabridged 1966 edition of *The Random House Dictionary of the English Language*.

Arthur C. Piepenbrink, supreme secretary of the Supreme Grand Lodge of AMORC (Ancient Mystical Order Rosae Crucis) of San Jose, California, publishers of *The Mystical Life of Jesus* and *The Secret Doctrines of Jesus*, both of which were written by the late Imperator of the Rosicrucian Order, H. Spencer Lewis, F.R.C., Ph.D.

Theodore Heline, executive director of the New Age Press, Inc., now of Oceanside, California, publishers of *The New Age Bible Interpretation*.

Lawrence Merkel, manager of the Theosophical University Press, Pasadena, California, publishers of the 1960 edition of *Isis Unveiled* by H. P. Blavatsky.

Mrs. Mary Bailey, president of Lucis Trust, and the Lucis Publishing Company, New York, N.Y., publishers of the books of Alice A. Bailey, including *Discipleship in the New Age; Initiation, Human and Solar;* and *A Treatise on the Seven Rays*.

Manly P. Hall, president and founder of The Philosophical Research Society, Inc., of Los Angeles, California, publishers of *An Encyclopedic Outline of Masonic, Hermetic, Qabbalistic and Rosicrucian Symbolical Philosophy*, of which work Mr. Hall is the author.

To all of the above, I send thoughts from the heart.

H. B. Dickey

July 25, 1969

Bibliography

Bailey, Alice A. *Discipleship in the New Age,* Vol. II. New York: Lucis Publishing Company.

———. *Initiation, Human and Solar.* New York: Lucis Publishing Company.

———. *A Treatise on the Seven Rays,* Vol. I, III. New York: Lucis Publishing Company.

Blavatsky, H.P. *Isis Unveiled,* Vol. I, II. Pasadena, Calif.: Theosophical University Press, 1960.

———. *The Secret Doctrine,* 3d. ed., Vol. I, II, III. London: Theosophical Publishing House London Ltd., 1928 (reprint).

Budge, E. A. Wallis. *Osiris, the Egyptian Religion of Resurrection,* Vol. I, II. New Hyde Park, N.Y.: University Books, Inc., 1961 (reprint).

Hall, Manly P. *An Encyclopedic Outline of Masonic, Hermetic, Qabbalistic and Rosicrucian Symbolical Philosophy,* 11th ed. Los Angeles, Calif.: Philosophical Research Society. Inc.

Holy Bible, The. Authorized (King James) Version.

Lewis, H. Spencer. *The Mystical Life of Jesus.* San Jose, Calif.: Supreme Grand Lodge of AMORC, Inc., 1929.

———. *The Secret Doctrines of Jesus.* San Jose, Calif.: Supreme Grand Lodge of AMORC, Inc., 1937.

New Age Bible Interpretation, The, Vol. IV. Oceanside, Calif.: New Age Press, Inc.

Random House Dictionary of the English Language, The, 1966 unabridged ed. New York: Random House, Inc.

Spence, Lewis. *An Encyclopaedia of Occultism.* New Hyde Park, N.Y.: University Books, Inc.